AI-Powered eCommerce

Elevating Customer Experiences, Optimizing Operations

A Comprehensive Guide by an eCommerce Expert - Strategies, Trends, and Use Cases

MICHAEL VAX

Table of Contents

Introduction

"It's hard to overstate how big of an impact AI will have on society over the next 20 years."

Jeff Bezos, Founder of Amazon

Machine Learning (ML) and Artificial Intelligence (AI) have been on an incredible journey. It started from theoretical concepts introduced in the middle of the 20th century to become an integral part of modern business environments. Now, it is not just the domain of the tech-savvy geeks. It's a technology that every business needs to understand and consider its far-reaching impacts on its future. The days when AI was an experimental side project are behind us.

Today, AI touches every industry and business function. It brings smarter decisions, better customer understanding, and unprecedented efficiencies. The business case for AI in eCommerce is convincing; it's inevitable.

AI poses ethical, societal, and even existential threats. But there's a corresponding opportunity for every challenge - a chance to leverage AI for business growth and human progress. We need to adopt an optimistic approach to AI's future.

eCommerce is an established industry. It continues to develop and grow, but its main techniques and approaches are already well-established and known. While we continue to see a steady pace of innovation, it has been a while since the industry experienced a ground-shaking change, like the mobile revolution, when merchants needed to rethink many entrenched concepts and implement substantial changes to stay competitive and relevant to their customers.

We have reached another critical point in eCommerce development - the general availability of powerful Artificial Intelligence tools that will profoundly affect eCommerce. It is that type of moment!

Remember when the first online businesses discovered and mastered SEO and dominated the online landscape?

Early adopters of AI have a unique opportunity to achieve an even bigger impact by applying Artificial Intelligence in their eCommerce operations. Leaving behind the media buzz, they need to understand the principles behind AI and the opportunities they offer in eCommerce to make informed decisions that leverage these technologies for strategic advantage. The future of AI is here; it's now for us to shape and steer how this technology is used in online business. Let's roll up our sleeves and work to create an intelligent, innovative business environment that utilizes the power of AI while respecting our human values. As Marc Andreessen said, It's time to build.

This book aims to serve as your compass, guiding your exploration of the strategic implications of Artificial Intelligence for an online business. It's not a technical manual or a list of step-by-step instructions. Look at it as a toolkit designed to aid you, eCommerce Professionals, in extracting the best from what AI offers to enhance and, in some areas, revolutionize the eCommerce industry. AI is a catalyst to help us build more innovative, resilient online businesses in this transformative time.

It is a critical technology for eCommerce companies seeking to remain competitive in today's environment. The benefits of applying AI are far-reaching, from operations and customer service to marketing. These benefits include improved efficiency of backend operations and staff satisfaction, better decision-making, and a more remarkable customer experience.

Artificial intelligence is a catalyst for innovation. It is encouraging new business models and creating new revenue streams on a level that mobile and social media revolutions have done in the past. It will boost bottom-line and top-line performance.

One of the key benefits of AI in eCommerce is its ability to enhance, change, and, in some cases, reinvent the customer experience. Imagine the most personalized and satisfying shopping experience in your life. I bet it was during in-person shopping when talking to a knowledgeable and attentive salesperson, not sitting in front of the computer and browsing a website.

Or what is the most natural way to order food when you want to know how spicy a dish is, the size of the portion, or how many starters to order for five people? Answering these questions when browsing a food delivery service website is challenging, while asking a waiter in a restaurant is so easy and convenient.

Humans are designed for conversation, not mouse movements and keyboard typing, and advances in Conversational AI will help us return to this profoundly natural way of product discovery and shopping.

By leveraging AI-powered personalization techniques, companies gain deeper insights into customer sentiment to provide highly targeted product recommendations and improved search results. With accurate machine

7

learning models, eCommerce teams can reduce the time customers take to make up their minds and finalize a purchase. They will help merchants better understand customer behavior and deliver accurate and targeted product recommendations by leveraging AI algorithms to analyze shopping and browsing history. These advancements increase shopping conversion rates and order values, and improve customer satisfaction.

With its ability to analyze vast quantities of data, AI will help marketers define more precise customer segments and improve the efficiency of advertising campaigns.

In addition to revolutionizing customer experience in eCommerce, another significant advantage of AI is its potential to maximize profitability.

Manual operational processes can often fall short in an industry where speed is vital. AI accelerates operational efficiency by automating new product onboarding, demand forecasting, merchandising, and content optimization tasks. Advanced machine learning models can achieve human-level accuracy and quality and augment human expertise with AI capabilities.

In today's digital commerce, AI has become an indispensable tool for online merchants and retailers seeking to meet evolving customer expectations, drive growth, and maintain market differentiation. It plays a central role in ensuring trust and safety by detecting and removing content that violates brand guidelines or damaging fake reviews.

The advantages of AI over human counterparts are evident in areas such as data analytics, forecasting, and image recognition, as well as spotting hidden trends and inconsistencies in data and processes. It works consistently with unparalleled speed, unaffected by distractions or fatigue.

Adopting Artificial Intelligence is no longer a choice; it has become a necessity in the eCommerce industry. Companies are leveraging AI to transform customer engagement, optimize online checkout processes, and streamline operations for digital commerce.

Throughout this book, you will get a comprehensive overview of the key applications of Artificial Intelligence in eCommerce and the opportunities it creates to enhance the customer experience, increase revenue, and improve backend operations. We will explore various AI techniques and their practical implementations, empowering you to harness the power of AI and stay ahead in the ever-evolving world of eCommerce.

Thank you for joining me, and let's approach this journey with informed optimism, curious minds, and a readiness to learn, experiment, and adapt.

How this book is Organized

This book is written to serve as your guide for navigating the complex landscape of Artificial Intelligence applications in online commerce. It is written to aid eCommerce professionals in understanding the multiple ways Artificial Intelligence can benefit an online business and how to unlock its full potential.

In contrast to some recent AI content that focuses on attention-grabbing topics, I want to give you a comprehensive view of how AI can enhance different aspects of Online Commerce. I aim to show approaches, tools, and techniques that you can work with now and, more importantly, provide you with a framework that you could use today, tomorrow, and in the future to decide where to apply AI in your business.

Rather than organizing the content around different AI technologies, the book structure revolves around the varied facets of the eCommerce business domain, encompassing both internal operations and shoppers' journeys and experiences.

The book consists of two parts.

It begins by analyzing how AI can revolutionize eCommerce customer experiences. We'll dive into the complex topic of eCommerce Search and Product discovery to examine how AI will transform it. We will explore Conversational Commerce, Virtual Shopping assistants, the integration of Augmented Reality (AR), Generative Personalization, and AI-based fraud prevention – each of these topics dissected to reveal AI's transformative influence.

The journey continues with Part 2, where you'll gain a deep understanding of AI's role in bolstering operational efficiency. It is important to emphasize that many backend enhancements fostered by AI will not only increase backoffice staff productivity but also lead to better customer experience, increased conversion rates, and revenue.

We discuss the AI impact on the Backend Operations of eCommerce organizations. Here, the spotlight is on how AI contributes to optimizing processes behind the scenes, from refining eCommerce Product Catalog preparation to automating merchandising and marketing activities, churn prediction, dynamic pricing, and enhancing demand and inventory forecasting.

But it doesn't stop there. We'll also explore how AI empowers non-technical employees to streamline their internal processes using AI-enabled code generation and no-code/low-code tools – a true testament to AI-driven skills democratization. That offers excellent opportunities for online merchants to reduce their IT expenses while further automating internal processes.

In the book's concluding chapters, I offer actionable recommendations on how to apply AI tools and approaches to your eCommerce businesses. They will guide you in crafting a customized AI roadmap by balancing the ambition and feasibility of currently available solutions. I will show you how to build AI literacy within your organization to foster collaboration, ensure effective implementation, and monitor future development as we are just at the early stages of this exciting journey.

Navigating AI technology choices can be complex. I will assist you by providing insights into selecting the right tools, software platforms, and partnerships aligned with your objectives.

While working on the "AI in eCommerce" training course and writing this book, I constantly researched currently available solutions, case studies, and future product announcements. I set up Google alerts on AI news and monitored eCommerce-related announcements from eCommerce vendors. During the last several months, there has been an explosion of new product developments and announcements. It is like the genie is out of the bottle and started to conquer the world.

As it usually happens with all new and exciting technology developments, there is a lot of surrounding marketing hype, repletion of old ideas, or rephrasing the same concepts. But I also saw many new innovative products and functionality released or announced by emerging startups and established eCommerce giants.

I included a description of selected innovative solutions in this book. My goal is twofold. Some of these solutions are already available and can be used to innovate and apply AI benefits in an eCommerce business. Don't wait! Use them to step ahead of your competitors.

But it is not only that. These AI pioneers demonstrate the possibilities for entrepreneurial businesses to significantly increase productivity and enhance customer experience. By offering a tangible glimpse into the potential of Artificial Intelligence, they will inspire you, readers, to envision and craft your own solutions that will captivate your customers and drive your business forward.

By imagining what is possible, you will be on a lookup for future, even more powerful AI systems that will revolutionize our industry.

Why I wrote this book

My eCommerce journey kicked off in 2008 when I stepped into the role of Chief Technology Officer at ElasticPath, a prominent Canadian eCommerce software provider. From there, I leaped the map to Germany, where I dived into the world of product management at Hybris, a frontrunner in eCommerce technology (now known as SAP Commerce Cloud). Continuing on this path, I assumed the position of Vice President of Product at Spryker, yet another influential player in the eCommerce software arena.

Through this fortunate sequence of opportunities, I had the privilege to actively participate in and lead the product journeys of three major eCommerce platform companies that remain major players in the industry and are recognized by analysts.

Over these years, I had opportunities to develop eCommerce solutions catering to various industries, encompassing retail, manufacturing, telecommunications, finance, travel, and even governmental entities. These engagements granted me a unique insider perspective on the evolution of eCommerce and allowed me to learn from and collaborate with the brightest minds in the eCommerce space.

I worked with many B2C & B2B businesses, helping them to navigate the digital transition, offering strategic guidance, and devising innovative roadmaps to unlock their growth potential.

Addressing the Knowledge Gap in the eCommerce Industry

Having worked closely with many clients, I realized that in a lot of organizations, the success of digital initiatives is hindered by the lack of eCommerce proficiency and knowledge.

While these companies have talented professionals well-versed in their specific industries and attuned to customer needs, the realm of eCommerce often remains uncharted territory, and a notable void often exists when it comes to the specialized expertise required for eCommerce implementation and operations.

Businesses want to move swiftly, yet they are entangled in delays due to the shortage of in-house experience. The lack of skilled people also often leads to implementing sub-optimal solutions.

To address this challenge, I founded CommerceIsDigital.com[1] with a clear goal: to create comprehensive training programs tailored to B2C and B2B eCommerce, effectively addressing this pressing skill gap.

The courses I offer are built upon a strong foundation of eCommerce knowledge. They include many practical examples and tried-and-true strategies from various industries and businesses, ensuring a well-rounded learning journey.

I feel proud that training helped hundreds of professionals become eCommerce experts.

Why AI in eCommerce?

AI has been a familiar companion in the eCommerce domain for quite a while now, and I've been covering its many applications within my courses. However, in the past several months, the advent of Generative AI has ignited a wildfire of new possibilities and avenues for AI in eCommerce.

While eCommerce is still actively evolving, its main components and flows are mainly established, and we see mostly incremental developments, probably, except for some B2B use cases. We have not had a big, revolutionary moment like mobile commerce in a while.

Like many people in the industry, I was curious about different use cases for Artificial Intelligence in eCommerce and soon realized that a comprehensive analysis is needed to understand AI's impact fully. Over time, what started as a personal research project morphed into online training and this book – a comprehensive exploration of the topic of AI in Ecommerce based on several months of intensive research.

My intimate familiarity with the eCommerce landscape gave me a unique vantage point and enabled me to envision AI's monumental potential within the eCommerce industry.

Glimpsing forward, I foresee a world where AI becomes an empowering tool for large and small merchants, enabling them to create remarkable value through abundant intelligence. While we're not quite at the point of Artificial General Intelligence (AGI), the current form of AI is already brimming with potential. Let's explore it together.

Understanding AI Concepts and Technologies

"Artificial intelligence is the science of making machines smart."

Dr. Fei-Fei Li - American computer scientist, Co-Director of the Stanford Institute for Human-Centered Artificial Intelligence

Artificial Intelligence (AI) is a vast and intricate field encompassing various technologies that enable computers to execute tasks that generally require human intelligence. These tasks include perception, reasoning, learning, and decision-making, accomplished using algorithms and statistical models that analyze data and make predictions or decisions based on the analysis, also known as machine learning.

One recent and prominent example of an AI application is ChatGPT - a human-like language model capable of generating unique and original content. It has gained significant media attention thanks to its accuracy and wide range of applications. Though important, it is crucial to remember that ChatGPT represents only a small fraction of generative AI in the broader AI landscape.

Artificial intelligence has become a game-changer in various industries, and eCommerce is no exception. With the rapid growth of eCommerce, merchants are constantly researching new ways to improve customer experience and optimize operations. AI has appeared as a powerful tool to help achieve these goals. However, understanding the underlying research and design principles is crucial for businesses to leverage it effectively in eCommerce.

Machine Learning

Machine learning (ML) is a part of AI that uses training to learn from data and make predictions or decisions. In eCommerce, ML can be applied to various aspects, such as predicting customer behavior, optimizing pricing strategies, and managing inventory. For instance, ML algorithms can analyze historical sales data to find patterns to predict future demand for merchant products. This information helps businesses reduce the risk of stockouts or overstocking.

One of the crucial components of AI is foundational models. Foundational models are general-purpose models (that can be used to solve many different use cases) pre-trained on massive amounts of diverse data. For example, Chat GPT was trained on over 45 terabytes of data or approximately 23 billion pages of plain text.

Foundational models serve as the building blocks for more specialized models and are based on three primary types of machine learning: Supervised Learning, Unsupervised Learning, and Reinforcement Learning.

Supervised Learning

The prime use of Supervised machine learning is to make predictions from data. First, we need to know what to predict. That is called the target value. Supervised Learning needs labeled (categorized) datasets to teach algorithms to categorize data and correctly predict outcomes. For example, Supervised Learning can help to predict the prices of houses. To do that, we will train the model using various characteristics, such as the house size, the number of bedrooms, the neighborhood, and, of course, the price of the house, which is the variable that needs to be predicted. After the training, the model can be used to predict prices and sales trends based on characteristics used in training.

Supervised Learning can address two distinct kinds of problems: Regression and Classification.

Classification problems require examples to be classified into one or more classes (categories). For example, they predict if a student will fail or pass a test based on their past performance. So, the output of the prediction will be pass or failed values.

Regression is solving problems in which the output is a variable number. The house price prediction example is an example of a regression problem. And, if we return to the student example, predicting a student's score on an exam gives us another example of a regression problem.

In eCommerce, product recommendation systems are notable examples of Supervised Learning.

One of the drawbacks of Supervised Learning is that required information may not be readily available or is costly to obtain and maintain.

Unsupervised Learning

Quite often, businesses accumulate large sets of unorganized, unlabeled data. Such data sets cannot help to determine what to predict as they have no labels or target values. While there are no apparent patterns in it, machine learning can help to discover some hidden relations and valuable information.

Here is where Unsupervised Learning comes in. It shines when people are unsure what they are looking for in data. Unsupervised Learning is searching for unknown trends, similarities, or differences in data.

It predicts the outcomes by studying the underlying patterns. In eCommerce, an example of the application of Unsupervised Learning is categorizing customers based on their buying behavior or social media activities.

Reinforcement Learning

When data scientists create an environment for an algorithm to learn independently, it is called Reinforced Learning. These models gained more popularity in recent years and produced significant results.

Reinforcement Learning does not require labeled data or a training set and is neither supervised nor unsupervised. Instead, it monitors the response to the actions of a learning agent.

Reinforcement Learning is a technique employed in areas like gaming and robotics. It involves a learning agent, which begins at a starting point and aims to reach a designated endpoint. The agent explores various paths to achieve this goal. Through interactions with its environment, the agent earns rewards for successful outcomes, while no rewards are given for failures.

For example, Amazon uses Reinforcement Learning to teach warehouse robots to pick up and move goods. Reinforced Learning is also used to optimize Dynamic Pricing algorithms by considering the associations between different pricing strategies and business outcomes.

Deep Learning

Deep Learning, a more advanced form of ML, also makes waves in eCommerce. It involves training AI models to recognize patterns and make decisions, similar to how the human brain works. Deep Learning works great for image recognition, which is particularly relevant for eCommerce businesses that rely heavily on visual content. With these algorithms, eCommerce platforms can automatically tag and categorize product images, making it easier for customers to find what they want. Additionally, it can be used to develop advanced recommendation systems that consider various factors, such as customer preferences, browsing history, and social media activity.

Natural Language Processing

Natural Language Processing (NLP) allows computers to understand and generate text and is an essential discipline of AI for eCommerce. Using products powered by NLP algorithms, eCommerce platforms can answer customer queries, provide personalized product recommendations, and even automate customer support using intelligent chatbots. NLP can help analyze customer reviews and feedback, enabling businesses to identify trends and understand customer requests.

Language models are used to generate content, implement chatbots, or automatic translations. They are trained to generate text that is similar to natural human language and rely on a range of technologies:

- Natural Language Understanding (NLU) allows machines to interpret and respond to human language, enabling applications like chatbots and virtual assistants.
- Speech-to-text technology empowers machines to transcribe spoken words into text, allowing people to dictate texts for machines to transcribe meetings and conversations.
- Text translation technology allows machines to translate text from one language to another.
- Text-to-speech technology converts written text into spoken language.
- Text-to-text technology generates new text based on input, allowing for automated summarization and content generation applications.

Computer Vision

Computer Vision models enable machines to interpret and analyze visual data from the world around them, including images and videos. They are based on four core technologies: image recognition, object detection, image segmentation, and image generation.

- Image recognition involves training models to recognize objects, scenes, and image patterns, e.g., recognizing customer faces to virtual try-on glasses.
- Object detection involves identifying and localizing objects within images or videos, e.g., locating windows and walls in a room to try different paint options.

16

- Image segmentation is a method of dividing an image into multiple parts, each corresponding to a different object in the image. For example, it can identify specific structures, such as a fashion garment, within an image.
- Image generation involves training models to generate new images. This technique is commonly applied in gaming and fashion to generate images of people, cars, and other items.

In eCommerce, computer vision models power virtual and augmented reality applications, like a virtual fitting room or placing furniture in a customer's living room.

In addition to language and computer vision models, a diverse range of specialized models are designed to perform specific tasks. These models are trained on large datasets of given data types, such as text, images, or video, and are fine-tuned for targeted use cases. The models can potentially automate complex processes and hence revolutionize entire industries.

In eCommerce, specialized models can be developed to detect fraud or fake reviews, optimize inventory management, predict product demand, or improve delivery routes.

PART I
REVOLUTIONIZING CUSTOMER
EXPERIENCE WITH AI

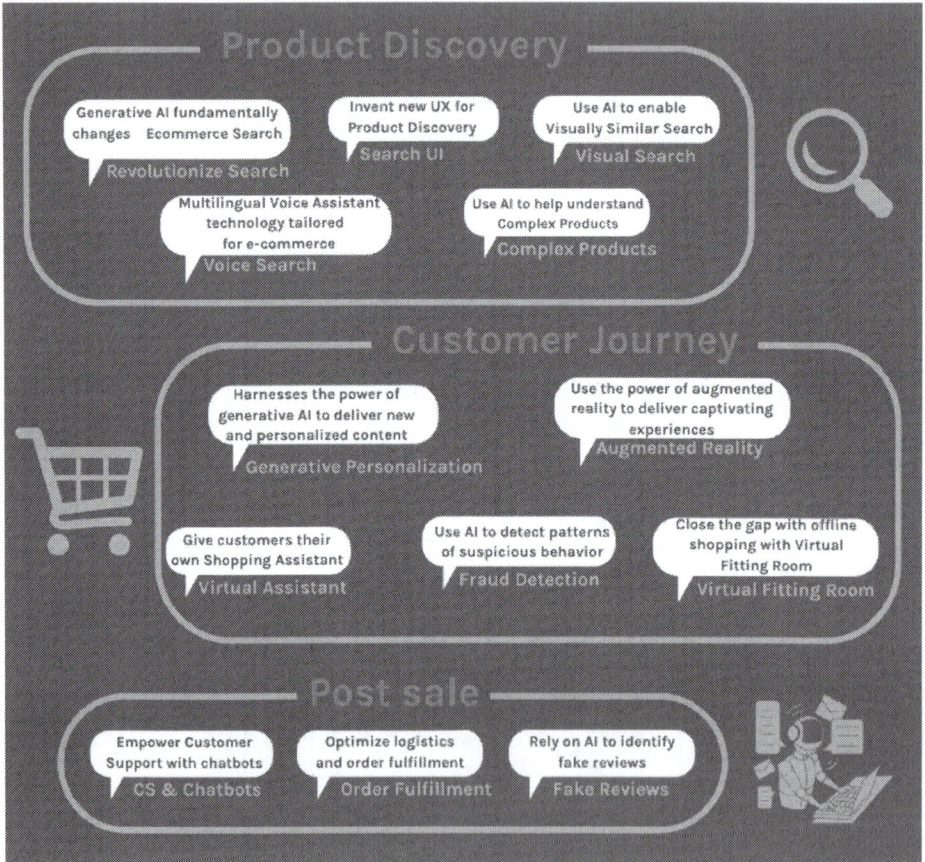

Product Discovery

Generative AI fundamentally changes Ecommerce Search
Revolutionize Search

Invent new UX for Product Discovery
Search UI

Use AI to enable Visually Similar Search
Visual Search

Multilingual Voice Assistant technology tailored for e-commerce
Voice Search

Use AI to help understand Complex Products
Complex Products

Customer Journey

Harnesses the power of generative AI to deliver new and personalized content
Generative Personalization

Use the power of augmented reality to deliver captivating experiences
Augmented Reality

Give customers their own Shopping Assistant
Virtual Assistant

Use AI to detect patterns of suspicious behavior
Fraud Detection

Close the gap with offline shopping with Virtual Fitting Room
Virtual Fitting Room

Post sale

Empower Customer Support with chatbots
CS & Chatbots

Optimize logistics and order fulfillment
Order Fulfillment

Rely on AI to identify fake reviews
Fake Reviews

Customer Experience Reimagined

"AI is not just about creating smarter machines, it is about creating a smarter world."

Andrew Ng, Founder of Google Brain.

The most profound impact of Artificial intelligence in eCommerce will be the transformation of the customer experience. Expect a broad spectrum of changes ranging from enhancements to existing customer journeys to full reinvention of how consumers discover and purchase products. The AI revolution will reshape the eCommerce industry and open a new era of innovation.

Imagine an eCommerce journey that goes beyond mere recommendations and becomes interactive. Picture yourself engaging in conversation with a virtual shopping assistant, sharing your needs, preferences, budget, and all the factors influencing your decision-making process. In response, this knowledgeable helper guides you through product catalogs, provides personalized recommendations, and offers additional suggestions and relevant product content. AI-driven recommendation systems analyze your browsing and purchase history, delivering recommendations that match your preferences.

Envision a shopping experience tailored just for you, where your search results align with your preferences, and you can find products that perfectly match your tastes using voice and visual search. AI-powered virtual assistants are here to make your shopping seamless. These intelligent bots enrich your experience by delivering real-time support.

Trying on clothes while shopping online becomes effortless with virtual fitting rooms powered by AI. Augmented Reality (AR) lets you visualize how products fit and look. Whether furniture or clothing, AR helps you make informed decisions, discover new products, and enjoy a curated shopping experience.

AI is transforming eCommerce by enhancing convenience and engagement.

Search & Product Discovery with AI

"The ultimate search engine would understand everything in the world, and it would always give you the right thing. And you wouldn't even have to ask for it."

Larry Page, Co-founder of Google

Search as the Core Engine of eCommerce

All modern eCommerce implementations rely on search to display products. And not only the search results page. Search also powers Product Listing (Categories) pages. eCommerce site search engines must be smart enough to recognize product names, categories, and product attributes and do it in multiple languages. They also should know synonyms, ignore cases, understand syntax, and more. Typos can and are happening, especially when it comes to brand names. Even if a merchant carries the brand, users may be unable to find it if there's a spelling error in the search query.

Studies show that search is the most used feature in an online store, and visitors who use search are up to 5–6 times more likely to convert than the shoppers who don't! But, it is not easy to get eCommerce Search right. It requires the right tools, expertise, and effort.

When a customer can't find what they've searched for on a website, whether or not it exists, they assume the brand does not have it (online or in-store), often leaving with no guarantee they will return. 76% of customers report abandoning a retailer after failing to find what they are searching for, with 48% purchasing the item elsewhere. More than half report [2] they typically abandon their entire shopping cart after failing to find a single item on a website. Eighty-five percent of consumers say they view a brand differently after experiencing search difficulties, and 77% avoid websites with poor search experiences[3].

Customers are not alone in acknowledging the extensive problem of bad site search; retailers agree. 90% of US-based website managers surveyed have identified the cost of search abandonment to their business as a serious concern.

Discovery on the Internet has come to rely on search and recommendation technologies for fast and intuitive information retrieval.

While legacy keyword search has worked well enough, it still suffers from inherent flaws associated with exact token matching and a maze of rules that overfit specific outcomes, which invariably create downstream problems for alternate use cases. These issues are exacerbated by messy and incorrect metadata in a product feed. Google estimates the cost of this problem to be worth $300bn per annum in the US alone.

About 43% of website users[4] opt to use the onsite search bar, and 94% of consumers say they receive irrelevant results when searching a retail website. Long tail queries are susceptible to poor or zero search results, and synonym-based approaches to relate edge queries to indexed product data fall short of understanding the context of the shopper's journey and intent behind his search requests.

These results prove that retailers have work to do to improve product search and discovery experience.

How Traditional eCommerce Search Works and Its Limitations

The cornerstones of data retrieval in search technology have been relational databases and keyword search engines. Keyword search operates on a principle of literal matching, pairing query terms with those in an indexed database, with techniques like Bag-of-Words (BoW) and Term Frequency-Inverse Document Frequency (TF-IDF) being the most common for ranking relevancy.

The TF-IDF value, for example, increases in direct proportion to the frequency of a word occurring in a document, balanced by the presence of the word in other documents within the corpus to help adjust for the fact that some words appear more frequently in general. This matching does not consider any meaning or context of the query. Instead, it is merely capable of identifying the exact match similarity of tokens or words. For this technology to work most effectively, two things must be true:

1. The retailer data set must be uniform, consistent, and complete.
2. The language, vocabulary, or jargon used to query must match that of the index.

That sounds simple. However, more often than not, retailers' data is not uniform, consistent, or complete. In addition, users prefer to conduct their searches in colloquial language, which often does not match the retailer data. Without the inference of meaning, the matching of words could be impossible.

Keyword search configuration is a laborious task, requiring an understanding of the website's unique user search behavior, knowledge of the corpus of data fields and tags in the context of their importance to a product, and technical understanding of how certain normalization, tokenization, and weighing should be applied to fields within the search index. Despite the amount of configuration that is done, there is still a reliance on token matching. In some cases, tokenization methods implemented to solve one problem or a use case create new problems for other queries.

Often, weights or 'boosts' are applied to specific categories or groups of products to combat poor results, conversely disappointing the retailer and the consumer when these products are ranked high in the results of what seems like an irrelevant query.

Due to the principle that keyword search relies upon the matching of tokens, this approach is incapable of grasping the nuanced meaning, context, or intent inherent in a user's query.

Synonyms libraries are the most common tool to circumvent this problem. For example, 'pants' and 'trousers' are synonymous to each other. However, that simple relationship must be manually mapped in keyword search. That extends to more complex relationships between words that are not synonyms but rather share meaning with each other. For example, 'lightweight', 'portable', 'small', 'mini', and 'travel' all might share the same meaning when referring to a 'camera tripod'. These same words, nevertheless, might not share meaning when referring to other items in the same retailer catalog. Terms such as 'travel bag' and 'mini bag' might refer to very different items, one designed with many compartments for a long trip and the other being compact and miniature.

The extent to which synonyms must be manually configured for keyword searches is far underestimated. In the case of words that share meaning only in specific contexts, a synonym library will only confuse queries where the meaning isn't shared.

URL redirects are used to manage explicit results to poor keyword matches, directing users to a listing or landing page related to their query. This practice can be a good quick fix when a retailer is struggling to accurately match and rank search results for a specific keyword; however, in almost all cases, doing this does not provide a list of results that match the query by relevance but rather a static page of specific products that require the user to filter further.

URL redirects and synonyms libraries help fix many of the underlying problems with relevancy in keyword searches today. Often, these tools are used to combat null search result keywords or the top-ranking keywords on a website. However, manually managing an extensive catalog at scale across thousands of search keywords faces limitations.

Improving eCommerce site search is an ongoing process of implementing data-driven changes to core search algorithms. Site search generates valuable data that merchants can utilize to learn and find the best algorithms and configurations to match those search queries with brand products to maximize conversion rates.

New AI Models Revolutionize eCommerce Search

While many eCommerce search queries today are just one to two words, younger people tend to search differently. They often use complete sentences and look for contextual results that match their intent. This shift requires a different approach to search that goes beyond keywords to understand the meaning of shopper's requests.

New Search Algorithms

Rather than matching keywords, new eCommerce search engines base their algorithms on Vector Search, which uses neural networks aided by natural language processing to analyze a query. Vector search uses distances in the embedding space to represent similarity. Finding related data becomes searching for the nearest neighbors of your query.

Vector embeddings are stored in multi-dimensional vectors and numerically represent data and related context. AI models that generate embeddings are trained on millions of examples to return more relevant and accurate results.

Vector embedding maps the words from the search to a corresponding vector to detect synonyms, intent, and ranking, and it clusters concepts to deliver more complete results. For example, the search query "fall wedding guest dresses for black tie event" would return relevant results for long dresses, dark colors, and sleeve options, even if the items weren't all tagged with the exact keywords.

The idea at the core of a vector search engine is that similar data and documents have matching vectors. Thus, when you use vector embeddings and index both queries and documents with them, you find similar documents as the closest neighbors of your search query.

Vector search powers semantic or similarity search. Since the meaning and context are captured in the embedding, we can understand what users mean with vector search without requiring a precise keyword match. And, it works with both textual data and images. It can handle longer search queries and reduce the return of "no results" compared to keyword search alone. That technique makes it easier for eCommerce sites to match buyer intent, personalize the shopping experience, and answer questions.

The vector models are also great for product recommendations as they learn to recognize similar documents and their vectors in the embedding space. For example, an application may recommend products that other shoppers who purchased the same item also liked.

Other metrics can be combined with Vector Distances to achieve multiple goals. For example, product recommendations can be ranked by revenue potential and satisfaction scores.

When natural language processing (NLP) is combined with processing documents with text embeddings, AI models can deliver full-text answers to customers' questions. That approach spares users from examining lengthy manuals and empowers merchant teams to provide answers faster.

A question-answering transformer model can learn from the documents from the knowledge base and FAQ to return the best answer.

Generative AI technologies like ChatGPT will seismically impact eCommerce search because they solve the critical problem of accurately matching user search intent with the right product results.

Presently, eCommerce search is primarily keyword-based. For example, if I search "What computer should I get?" on Amazon, the top three results are a book by Ramit Sethy, "I Will Teach You to be Rich", a Lenovo laptop, followed by another book called "Shit I Can't Remember".

ChatGPT will fundamentally change the approach to search because its natural language processing system can understand user intent thanks to an unprecedented predictive model trained on nearly a trillion words.

Here's is the proof: When I type "What computer should I get?" in ChatGPT, I get a detailed bullet-point response with top considerations for choosing a computer, such as intended use, operating system, portability, budget, and technical characteristics like memory and display size.

ChatGPT understands what I'm trying to find.

Combining Publicly Available Information with Merchant's Data

Despite its strengths, ChatGPT does have limitations. One of its weaknesses is that it relies solely on publicly available information to train its language model. That means that when it comes to specific tasks like helping users choose a suitable computer, ChatGPT can only provide generic suggestions. It lacks the ability to personalize recommendations based on factors like pricing, popularity, and users' purchase history at the product level. To achieve such personalized recommendations, ChatGPT needs access to proprietary platform data from retailers.

The next significant leap to advance eCommerce search capabilities will involve combining the intent prediction power of generative AI with the vast amount of data available on eCommerce websites. By leveraging this combination, eCommerce companies can develop a next-generation search experience that accurately delivers search results based on both user intent and external information.

The ultimate goal of eCommerce search is to surface the right product for customers without them ever needing to resort to a third-party search engine. Generative AI represents a significant stride toward achieving this goal.

By harnessing the potential of generative AI, eCommerce companies can provide highly personalized and tailored search experiences, ensuring that customers find the products they desire seamlessly within the eCommerce platform itself.

New Search UX is to be Invented

We are all familiar with eCommerce search boxes. When implemented correctly, it employs search-as-you-type functionality, instantly displaying results and suggestions as the customer starts typing.

The search results usually encompass several elements:

- Categories matching the search terms.
- Relevant products and personalized recommendations.
- The search results may also include product-related content such as landing pages, manuals, or blog posts.

AI-powered search engines would utilize natural language processing (NLP) to process and comprehend queries. That enables the search engine to understand the meaning behind the query and present the most relevant and highly ranked search results.

These advancements in Generative AI will revolutionize eCommerce Search and reinvent the search user interface. Let's discuss how this can fundamentally change the search interface and user experience.

Presently, eCommerce websites have separate areas for search bars and chatbot interactions. It makes sense since product search relies on keyword matching, while chatbots respond to a limited set of natural language queries.

This separation often results in a clunky user experience, with chatbots typically placed in the bottom corner of the screen while the search bar is at the top of the page.

However, with the advent of generative AI, the search bar and chatbot can respond to the same set of natural language queries. This integration allows for a seamless union of the chatbot within the search bar, enabling it to assist in finding products as well as answering general, non-product-related questions.

Users would be able to utilize natural language in the eCommerce search bar. For instance, Amazon search now may not fully understand a query like "What books are in the Harry Potter series?". It may return irrelevant top results like a LEGO Marvel Spider-Man toy or a Star Wars encyclopedia. With generative AI, the search results will list the individual Harry Potter books in the correct sequence, eliminating the need for users to search for this information on external platforms.

Next-generation search will deliver advanced product recommendations. As discussed earlier, generative AI-powered eCommerce search will seamlessly integrate both on-platform data, such as product and user data, and off-platform data, such as social media signals and influencer product reviews.

While currently, eCommerce recommendations heavily rely on the retailer's own data, with generative AI, merchants will gain access to an extensive range of external data sources, augmenting on-platform data to provide significantly more relevant and personalized product recommendations. With these advancements, next-generation eCommerce Search will make the shopping experience seamless for customers, allowing them to find products tailored to their preferences.

Let's take a look at some examples of innovative product search and recommendation solutions to get a taste of upcoming advances enabled by artificial intelligence.

AI-powered Product Discovery Platform

Klevu[5] is one of the product discovery platforms for personalized search, merchandising, and recommendations. To improve the quality of the results, it processes and understands what the shoppers mean when they search in the context of the merchant's catalog.

Klevu AI focuses on linguistics and continuous machine learning to enhance users' shopping experiences. By parsing search queries and content, Klevu uses semantic search to understand intent and meaning and automatically presents the most relevant results.

Its human-centric Natural Language Processing (NLP) model is specifically designed for eCommerce with multilingual capabilities. It uses natural language processing and localized machine learning to determine what shoppers want in nearly any language. The cultural preferences are nuanced and impossible to get right and do at scale with manual merchandising. Klevu AI can learn automatically from local shoppers to prioritize products most likely to convert in each region.

Here is a simple explanation of how Klevu AI works. Merchants' product feed is sent to Klevu to be indexed by its NLP Enrichment Pipeline. User behavior analytics use a reinforced learning model by processing shoppers' clicks, purchases, and reviews. The Query Processing module preprocesses the shopper's search query to produce search results displayed on the eCommerce store, and the AI model processes customer behavior on the site to further personalize returned search results.

Size Recommendation Solutions

And here is an AI solution that all fashion brands would wish to have - a predictive AI-powered size recommendation system. Sizolution AI[6] combines customer data, garment data, and predictive AI to provide the best possible personalized recommendation.

Two AI technologies make Sizolution work. First is Automated Garment Measuring, which extracts size information from product images and significantly enhances the accuracy of garment measurements. The second captures a customer's full body image, which AI analyzes to create a personalized 'parametric body model', which can then be matched with individual products.

AI enables Sizolusion to produce size recommendations tailored specifically to each individual consumer, considering their unique body shape and size.

Voice Search

Voice search has rapidly gained popularity due to its natural and efficient communication method. It is poised to become one of the preferred ways for shoppers to search for information or place orders. Nature has designed us to speak, not type.

In traditional text-based searches, users tend to employ short, keyword-driven queries. However, with voice technology, users prefer longer, more conversational phrases resembling natural speech. As a result, businesses must optimize their websites to target long-tail keywords and cater to natural language search queries to ensure visibility in search results.

As voice search technology evolves, exciting opportunities emerge to integrate voice assistants into the shopping experience. That can include providing personalized recommendations or enabling customers to place orders using their voice effortlessly.

The rise of advanced language models like ChatGPT has paved the way for innovative startups that offer Multilingual Voice Assistant technology explicitly tailored for eCommerce shoppers. Such voice assistant empowers users to find answers to their questions seamlessly on the transaction screen, eliminating the need to switch to external search engines like Google. The voice assistants enhance the user experience and simplify the search process by leveraging the information within the eCommerce application and relevant external knowledge.

Also, the power of generative AI extends to popular voice assistants from Amazon or Google, further enriching the customer experience and driving sales. By integrating these platforms, direct-to-consumer (DTC) and eCommerce merchants can allow customers to purchase through their voice-enabled devices, creating a convenient and frictionless shopping experience.

The future of Voice Search holds tremendous potential for transforming how people interact with technology and make online purchases. Businesses that embrace voice optimization and leverage generative AI capabilities will be well-positioned to delight customers and stay ahead of competitors.

Preparing for Voice Search

How can merchants optimize for voice search?

Preparing eCommerce website and product listings for voice search can significantly enhance the customer experience, making it easier for them to discover products with voice commands. To accomplish this, consider implementing the following strategies:

1. Incorporate Long-Tail Keywords and Conversational Language

Unlike traditional text-based searches, voice search queries are often longer and resemble a natural conversation. Incorporate long-tail keywords that reflect the way people speak when asking questions or seeking information. Focus on phrases that begin with words like "Who," "What," "Where," "When," "Why," and "How." By aligning the content with these conversational phrases, merchants can increase the chances of their eCommerce site appearing in voice search results.

2. Address Frequently Asked Questions

Create an FAQ area on the website to address customers' common questions. Write the answers in a conversational tone, mimicking how users might ask the questions. That approach helps with voice search optimization and provides valuable information to potential customers, improving their overall experience on the site.

3. Optimize Product Descriptions and Titles

Ensure that product descriptions, titles, and category tags contain relevant details that align with user queries. Include specific attributes, such as color, size, gender, or other relevant information, to make it easier for voice search algorithms to match user intent with your products. For example, a descriptive title like "Blue sports T-shirt with V-neck for female, size 36" would be well-suited for voice search.

4. Leverage AI for Voice Recognition

With advancements in AI, voice recognition technology has improved, allowing for a better understanding of user voices, including distinguishing between male and female voices. Take advantage of this capability by tagging any "gender-specific" items accordingly. By properly labeling products, such as specifying if they are designed for men or women, retailers can enhance the accuracy of voice search results and improve the relevance of product recommendations.

By implementing these optimization strategies, an online store can effectively cater to voice search users, ensuring they can find the information and products they need quickly and easily. The adoption of voice technology for eCommerce search will grow rapidly, powered by new advances in AI. Merchants need to make sure they are ready for it.

Visual Search

Visual search is an innovative feature gaining traction in eCommerce sites, aiming to attract more customers. This cutting-edge technology leverages artificial intelligence to enable shoppers to search online using images rather than text or keywords.

With visual search, shoppers can skip the need to describe an item and instead snap a picture or share an image from social media. By uploading it to a visual search engine, merchants can quickly find similar products.

While traditional visual search is still relatively new, the next evolution of search is emerging in the form of Visually Similar Search. This advanced approach allows shoppers to crop an image and select specific attributes like shape, color, or pattern, leading to recommendations tailored more closely to their preferences.

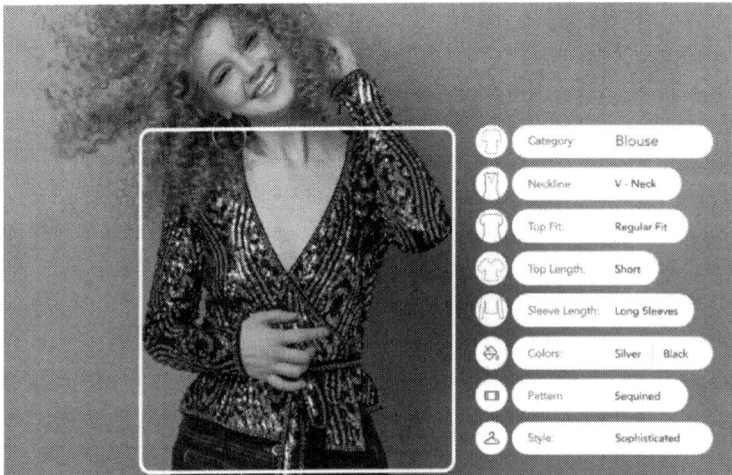

Source: pixyle-ai

Powered by AI and machine learning, Visually Similar Search instantly connects users with the items they're looking for. Searching by image returns hyper-personalized results, delivering a customized user journey to explore the brand's website and products. It provides customers with comprehensive access to a range of relevant products, creating an immersive product discovery capability that drives conversions.

ViSENZE is an AI Search and Discovery company implementing a powerful Visual Search solution. With ViSENZE[7], merchants can embed visual search capabilities into online store search bars, mobile Apps, or Chatbot interactions. A camera icon appears in all these places, letting shoppers quickly snap or download a picture as part of their search request.

Visual AI Search solution will identify the product in the image. If the exact match is unavailable, the system can recommend similar products based on visual similarity, color, and style relevance.

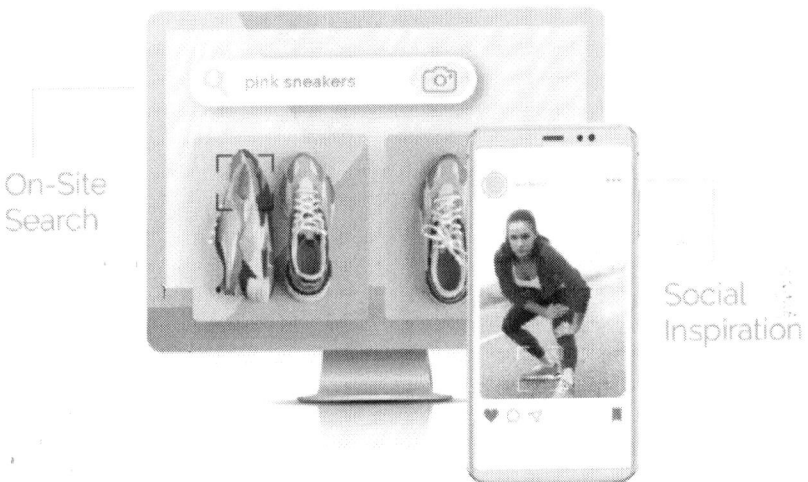

Source. Search Bar Integrated with ViSENZE

Using AI to Discover Complex Products

With more and more transactions moving online, we should be able to sell any product digitally. But what about complex products and services? How do we make it easy for customers to buy complex products or services that require making several choices and adjusting multiple parameters to choose between thousands of combinations? And I am not talking about selecting a color and size that sellers can quickly solve with variants.

Merchants implement support for Configurable Products to enhance the user experience when buying complex products. A configurable product is a product that customers can change, configure, and personalize before it is purchased. If you can master the implementation of eCommerce for configurable products, there is no limit on what you can sell online.

In some cases, merchants also sell a complex combination of products and must guide customers through several steps to ensure they buy the correct combination. The selection process is usually broken into several steps, and the customer's choice in previous steps sometimes influences the options available in the next one. Merchants often need to implement validation rules required to ensure the correct configuration. The final price could also change based on the choices made during the configuration.

Selecting a complex product may represent a frustrating and time-consuming task. Customers often feel overwhelmed and need to invest considerable effort to become nearly experts in the field without the guarantee of finding the desired product in stock. At the same time, merchants and producers of such products lack an effective, customer-friendly way of presenting their offerings, potentially making customers feel lost or frustrated and abandoning their search.

Instead of forcing customers to become experts on filters and parameters, with the help of artificial intelligence, we can simply ask about their needs and turn product selection into an engaging conversation.

An example is the Czech start-up Outfindo[8], which provides a customer-product matching experience through a guided selling approach powered by AI. Initially focusing on bikes and e-bikes, the startup has now expanded its services to washing machines in collaboration with major eCommerce platforms.

By engaging customers in a conversation and asking simple questions, Outfindo's AI-driven discovery and sales tool assists in selecting products that meet their needs and narrowing down the options. According to Outfindo, its solution reaches a 40% interaction rate with the guide among visitors, boosts website conversions by up to 3 times, and reduces returns by up to 70%.

Key Takeaways: Search & Product Discovery

The product search and discovery landscape in eCommerce is poised for a revolutionary transformation by integrating AI technologies. The advent of natural language understanding and context-driven results has ushered in a paradigm shift. This evolution demands a novel approach to search, removing the confines of fixed keywords to move into the realm of intent and meaning.

AI tools are redefining the way customers explore and find products. They unlocked the potential for users to articulate their queries in full sentences, seeking results that align precisely with their intent. This shift resonates with a more intuitive and user-centric search experience, fundamentally altering how customers interact with online stores.

Yet, this transformation is only the tip of the iceberg. The journey toward enhanced eCommerce search capabilities is propelled by a synergy of two potent forces: generative AI's prowess in predicting user intent and the reservoir of user data available within eCommerce businesses. That holds the key to the next evolutionary leap. By harnessing the predictive abilities of generative AI alongside the wealth of user and product data, eCommerce companies can mold a new generation of search experiences.

- ☐ Seek out Search and merchandising vendors who have embraced these emerging capabilities and seamlessly integrated them into their solutions. That ensures you're poised to leverage the latest innovations in search technology to augment your customers' journey.
- ☐ Research different approaches to search user interfaces by combining search, visual search, and conversational capabilities of AI-powered chatbots.
- ☐ Using natural language capabilities, let customers engage with your platform using everyday language to bridge the gap between search queries and relevant results. The outcome will be a search experience that feels less like a transaction and more like a human conversation.
- ☐ But the journey doesn't end there. Consider the untapped potential of visual and voice search. Investigate how to seamlessly integrate these emerging technologies into your online store and introduce an entirely new dimension of convenience.

AI's role in elevating product search and discovery within eCommerce is undeniably transformative. The fusion of natural language understanding, predictive AI, and contextual results enriches the search experience and empowers customers to navigate the digital marketplace in ways that mirror real-world interactions. As the eCommerce industry continues to evolve, the journey of exploration, integration, and innovation in product search remains an exciting odyssey to embrace.

Bringing Personalization to the Next Level

"Technology should do the hard work so people can do the things that make them the happiest in life."

Larry Page, Co-founder of Google

In a world driven by constant connectivity, online experiences need to be more personalized than ever before. A highly customized approach must aim to create the most relevant and personalized experience for each user. Advanced personalization leverages technology and data analysis techniques to understand users' behaviors, preferences, and needs, resulting in tailor-made experiences that create highly relevant contextual interaction at the right moment of customers' journey.

AI hyper-personalization goes further than segmentation and allows brands to create a customer experience that is not only unique to an individual but is done in real time. Businesses that accomplish this will position themselves as attentive and responsive and achieve competitive differentiation in increasingly crowded markets. It will lead to increased conversion rates and customer loyalty.

That brings us to Generative Personalization. Imagine if AI could generate completely personalized content on demand. That's the promise behind Generative Personalization.

Generative Personalization harnesses the power of generative AI models to craft new and personalized content. Unlike traditional personalization methods that make recommendations based on past user behavior, generative personalization takes it a step further by producing entirely new content tailored to each individual at a specific moment of their journey.

Let's break down how to implement it.

To make Generative Personalization work, we need to have customer data and define a prompt template that serves as a framework. By merging these two elements, we create a Personalized AI prompt that acts as a brief for the AI. When we run the Personalized prompt, we unleash the AI's creative powers to generate unique output that can be stored for later use or utilized immediately.

Generative Personalization becomes a scalable solution with incredible potential by automating the process of selecting the appropriate prompt and populating a template with customer-specific data. It can be used with text or images.

Let's say we plan to use a stock photo - "man looking at his laptop". There are multiple ways we can use different customer and merchant data to personalize it.

Think about the possibilities and the personalization options we can get practically "for free" by filling customer data into the prompt template.

- You can change the Man's age.
- Select what to show on the laptop's screen (statistics, a presentation, or a family picture).
- Change office Location (view outside the window can be from the Netherlands, New York, or London).
- Make sure he has mineral water in the picture! (versus coffee, tea, or other beverages)
- You can also change the setting, time of the day, tone
- Combination of any of the above

"in the Netherlands"
"add cup of coffee"
"during evening"
"at the jaarbeurs"

Source: Email Monday[9]

The future of eCommerce is about to surpass anything we've witnessed so far. Generative AI is set to revolutionize the game, and we're just scratching the surface with examples like ChatGPT. This incredible technology holds immense potential to elevate the shopping experience to unparalleled heights, offering truly personalized, one-to-one interactions.

Generative AI will fuel dynamic messaging, real-time imagery tailored to customer's needs, and predictive recommendations. It is the first technology that allows merchants to achieve scalable personalization in a cost-effective manner that surpasses what humans alone could do. Dynamic pricing and promotions will further enhance the experience.

What's more, the localization aspect of generative AI empowers brands to adapt product descriptions and images to match regional preferences and cultural nuances. This fine-tuning ensures a seamless connection with diverse audiences, no matter where they are. Just imagine if product descriptions can be modified on the fly to include the words a customer used in her search.

Startup Cooee embarked on a mission to democratize AI for eCommerce, helping brands convert more visitors by real-time personalization.

COOEE[10] believes all customer journeys are unique and has developed a solution to deliver 1-on-1 personalization based on real-time intent. Instead of static rule-based campaigns to deliver pop-ups that annoy and disrupt shoppers, COOEE analyzes 40 plus micro behaviors in real time to understand where they are in their buying journey and engages with them using uniquely crafted content and offers.

AI analyzes merchant traffic to understand visitor intent and uses dynamic product listings and personalized messages to nurture low-intent customers and guide shoppers with medium intent. High-intent customers are greeted by name and presented with a personalized call to action with a generated unique coupon code.

The generative AI takes seconds to generate custom images and create unique product presentations based on customer behavior on the side, browsing and purchasing history, and cart content. It learns what customers prefer and creates altered design versions for each customer.

Key Takeaways: Personalization

- ☐ Merchants have access to multiple sources of information that can be leveraged to showcase products in the best possible way online. They need to break data silos and utilize all this available information from different contexts to deliver a truly dynamic and customized experience.

- ☐ Personalization has always been the holy grail of eCommerce, and we are getting closer to achieving it on an entirely new level that delivers 1-on-1 personalization at scale and cost-efficiently.

- ☐ Generative Personalization offers one of the best ways to differentiate the online experience for your customers.

AI-Assisted Shopping

The Resurgence of Conversational Commerce

The notion of Conversational commerce emerged from a 2015 Medium article by Uber's Chris Messina[11], delineating the fusion of messaging apps with the realm of shopping. Over time, this concept has broadened its horizons to encompass voice interactions, leveraging advancements in speech recognition technology.

Chatbots inevitably come to the forefront when discussing AI's impact on eCommerce. However, it's crucial to discern how AI-powered chatbots diverge from those annoying pop-ups that interrupt our browsing experience from the bottom right corner, often before we even get a chance to explore merchant's products.

The problem with traditional chatbots is they aren't built with true AI. They work on predefined rules vs. machine learning and natural language understanding. Customers only get an answer if they search exactly for what the chatbot is trained to find. Many need customers to use specific predefined vocabulary to give the correct answers, which can be frustrating if a visitor doesn't ask the question precisely how the chatbot requires.

New-generation chatbots support Conversational Commerce that leverages natural language processing and new machine-learning techniques to understand what a user is searching for. These bots allow shoppers to have conversations with the machine that is returning humanlike responses.

A chatbot powered by conversational AI uses contextual awareness and analyzes incoming customer queries to understand shoppers' sentiments and intent. That means shoppers are likelier to get their questions answered the first time they engage.

As the "conversation-first" future arrives, people's impression of one's brand will be affected by the bot's effectiveness, how much contextual value it has, and how fast it can deliver it. Conversations go nowhere unless people perceive them as valuable. The chatbots should be connected to a customer's shopping history, anticipate what they seek, and answer questions instantly through chat. They should be available 24/7 year-round and get smarter every day.

I cannot emphasize this enough! Quality of the Conversation experience affects human emotions and perception. When customers encounter a frustrating chatbot experience, their sentiments often spill over to affect how they perceive the brand.

Virtual Shopping Assistants

Armed with cutting-edge techniques like Natural Language Processing and machine learning, these conversational bots have become exceptionally adept at understanding us. They're like our personal problem-solving wizards, equipped to provide precise and relevant answers.

These virtual assistants don't just make shopping remarkable; they make it profoundly personal. It's like embarking on a shopping escapade with a trusted advisor by your side. Brands that give their customers this feeling of a trusted shopping companion experienced in products offered will enjoy delighted customers and amplified sales.

Technology allows merchants to create their very own branded AI shopping assistants. These virtual companions assume the voice and persona of the brand, skillfully guiding customers through the vast landscape of options, aiding in making informed choices, and addressing any burning inquiries they may have.

To capitalize on this trend, Walmart has created Text to Shop[12], a mobile app that introduced Conversational commerce to its customers. The application was developed by Walmart's incubator arm, Store No8. Shoppers can use the Text to Shop app to create shopping lists for a visit to a Walmart store or shop online to pick up their products at their nearest supercentre.

Two frequently used ways users communicate with brands online are by messaging them on Facebook and Instagram or going to their website and searching for a chat widget. It's imperative that brands meet their customers where they are and automate conversations to deliver instant value with every interaction, whether answering questions about shipping times or taking things further and asking questions, processing data, and returning product recommendations tailored to each individual's needs.

That brings us to another interesting AI startup - GROW AI[13]. It develops chatbots that let customers shop online via Facebook Messenger, Instagram, and WhatsApp. The chatbots collect real-time data on users' journeys, which helps to improve merchants' sales and marketing efforts.

Conversational AI allows the development of a seamless experience for consumers at every stage of their customer journey, whether converting a first-time visitor into a new customer, re-engaging them through different campaigns, or simply answering questions on the spot. It continues adding value to shoppers, increasing the retention rate.

Keeping track of conversation history, customer interests, and sentiment allows AI to understand customers and deliver a hyper-personalized experience, where the bot knows their entire purchase history and can act based on that data.

Zalando, a leading European online platform for fashion and lifestyle, uses a fashion assistant powered by ChatGPT across its mobile app and web platforms. Customers can ask questions using their own fashion terms, and the bot helps them intuitively navigate Zalando's large assortment.

For example, if a shopper asks, "What to wear for a wedding in Barcelona in August?" the assistant can understand that this is a formal event and what the weather is in Barcelona in August and gives recommendations followed by reasons behind them.

To deliver a more personalized range of products in future versions that could be combined with additional customer preferences, such as brands they follow, styles they prefer, and products available in their sizes. This technology introduces a new way to discover Zalando's assortment and provide customers with more intuitive fashion inspiration.

It is essential to find new innovative ways to integrate visual product selection right into chat conversations. Here is how it is done at Mercari, a second-hand goods marketplace in the US. As most of its products are unique, Mercari has a huge catalog and looked for ways to make it easier for customers to explore Mercari's extensive marketplace. A virtual shopping assistant, Merchat AI, was developed to address this challenge.

In the chat interface, customers explain to the bot what they are looking for and answer clarifying questions. AI will suggest some products for shoppers right in the chat interface, providing a smooth experience.

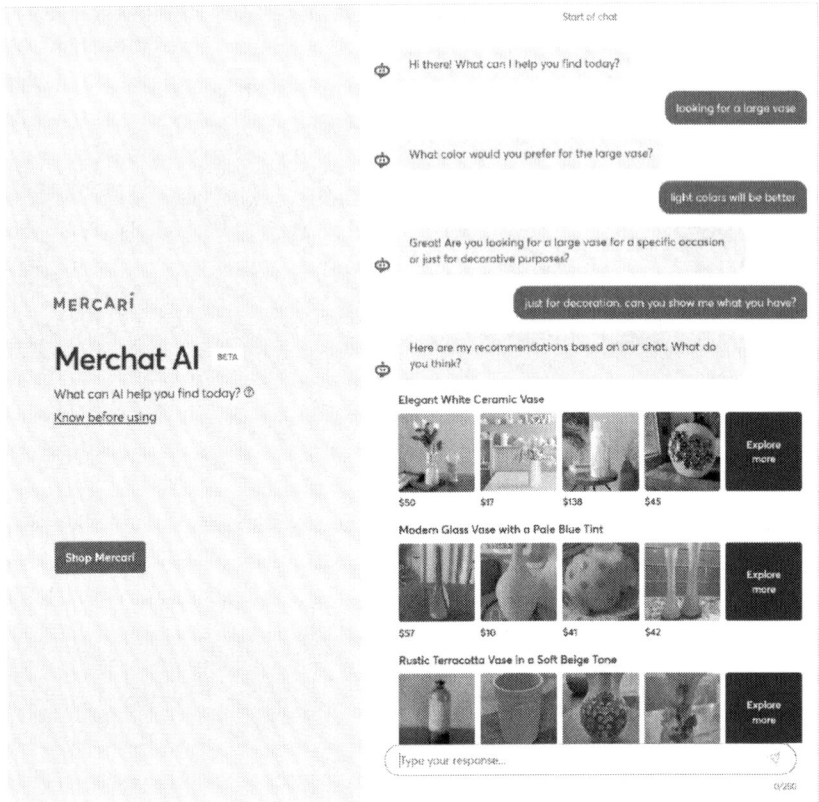

AI-powered chatbots can simulate human-like conversations and provide contextual, personalized experiences. That helps brands understand what their buyers want and return a further personalized customer experience with each interaction.

With conversation-based virtual assistants, merchants can transform the customer's online experience from mere convenience shopping to consultative commerce. This shift empowers online businesses to compete more effectively with brick-and-mortar stores.

Augmented Reality (AR)

"I think we are high on AR for the long run. I think AR is big and profound. This is one of those huge things that we'll look back at and marvel at the start of it."

Tim Cook, CEO of Apple

This technology has been around for some time, and with advancements in artificial intelligence, it is gaining broader adoption in the eCommerce industry. AR in eCommerce lets shoppers virtually try on products, such as clothing or jewelry, or place products virtually in a surrounding space. AR product visualization takes customer journeys to the next level and enhances the brand's image.

It not only increases customer engagement and satisfaction by providing a more interactive shopping experience but also reduces product return rates by offering customers a more accurate representation of products.

Virtual Fitting Room & Augmented Reality

With online shopping, trying on clothes in a fitting room is simply not an option. Instead, we rely on photos of models to imagine how a garment might look on us. But here's the catch: it's hard to visualize the fit accurately if we have different body types from the models. That discrepancy often leads to a significant number of returns, posing a challenge for eCommerce brands. According to the National Retail Federation, fit and size account for a whopping 42% of all online apparel returns.

To combat this issue and reduce eCommerce return rates, merchants can leverage the power of AI-driven virtual fitting rooms and virtual try-on technology. These innovative solutions allow customers to visualize a broad range of products, from footwear to clothing and jewelry, before making a purchase.

There are two primary approaches to implementing virtual fitting rooms. The first involves customers creating a 3D scan of their bodies using a mobile app, enabling them to virtually try on apparel using personalized 3D avatars.

The second approach offers a selection of different models with body types similar to the shoppers. Customers can choose a model that resembles them and see how an article of clothing would look on that model before making their buying decision. That is what Google has recently introduced as a new virtual try-on feature for Search, which utilizes the power of TryOnDiffusion[14], a generative AI developed by Google researchers. This advanced technology analyzes clothing images and predicts how they would look on various models, covering sizes from XXS to 4XL and various poses.

By incorporating augmented reality, retailers can accurately represent a customer's body and demonstrate how clothes will fit and look. In fact, according to Shopify, customers who utilized augmented reality software to try on clothing were found to be 40% less likely to return the item.

Following its acquisition of a virtual fitting room start-up, Zeekit, Walmart created a virtual try-on tool[15], "Be Your Own Model", which emulates an in-store fitting room experience for online shoppers. It enables customers to use their photos to visualize how the clothing will look on them. To use the feature, shoppers need to upload a picture of themselves in the Walmart app. After that, they can virtually try on any product from over 270,000 items across Walmart's catalog.

Merchants that cannot develop virtual fitting rooms in-house can evaluate software vendors like Geenee. [16]Geenee's solutions include full-body virtual try-on for products like T-shirts, dresses, skirts, pants, jackets, and sweaters and try-on for beauty products and accessories such as handbags, jewelry, glasses, hats, and other head-worn accessories.

Geenee offers a suite of solutions for online and offline retail stores. The main features include:

- eCommerce point of sale – web-based full body and face tracking, allowing customers to try all types of products, from head to feet;
- Onsite mirrors – AR mirrors[17] that allow customers to try on products in-store without going to a changing booth;

Another AR vendor for online commerce is Perfect Corp[18]. Using artificial intelligence, it has developed several solutions to create realistic augmented reality (AR) for fashion merchants.

The AgileHand™ tracking technology is ultra-precise 3D Hand Tracking Technology that helps brands use virtual try-ons on a wide range of products for a hand, including watches, bracelets, rings, nail polish, and press-on nails.

Shoppers can try it by going to the Perfect website and giving it access to a laptop camera.

Perfect Corp's Live 3D Face AR is a real-time facial detection technology that powers realistic facial mapping for accurate makeup trials. Using more than 100 facial points, the technology can detect wide-angle facial profiles, facial movements, and light changes, allowing for real-time hyper-realistic virtual makeovers.

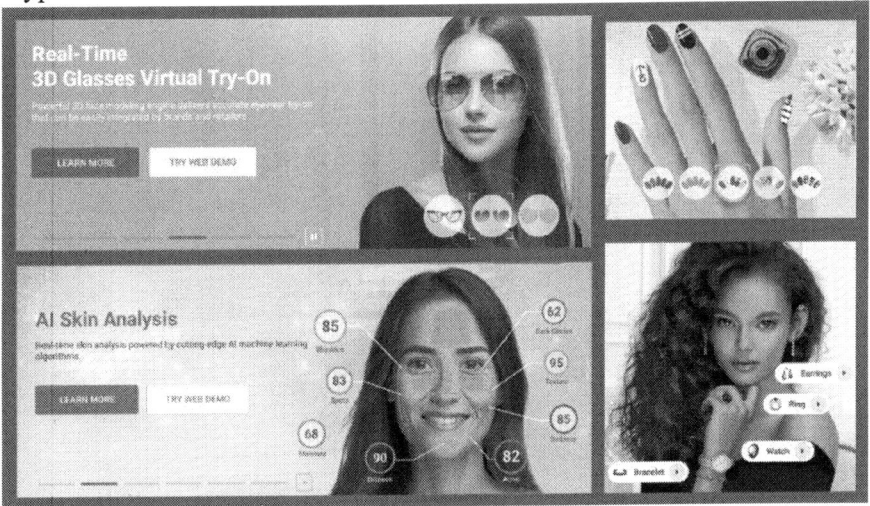

Source: Perfect Corp.

And the Skincare AR technology goes even further. The AI skin diagnostic tool uses deep learning technology to give users real-time skincare analysis. It tracks the efficacy of skincare over time using the "Skin Diary" feature by accurately detecting wrinkles, skin texture, and dark circles. That is a compelling example of AR's potential to shift customer relationships from transactional to long-lasting by continuously delivering value and enhancing their lives.

AR "try-on" solutions redefine shopper experience, breaking the barriers of traditional retail locations and bringing products to life in the digital land. As this technology continues to evolve, businesses have a unique opportunity to establish stronger connections with their customers and a competitive edge.

Another exciting opportunity is to combine an AR solution with a live shopping experience to give customers personalized guidance from a knowledgeable salesperson, replicating the in-store shopping experience.

Elevating eCommerce with Augmented Reality

Augmented reality (AR) has more to offer in eCommerce than just virtual fitting rooms. By employing AR technology, merchants can provide their customers with immersive, interactive shopping experiences that would genuinely captivate them.

Take IKEA's AR app as an inspiring example. Through this app, customers can visualize how IKEA furniture would look in their own spaces before selecting a product, capture pictures of desired home pieces, and discover similar products. Another remarkable example is Tap Painter, an AR app that empowers users to virtually paint their rooms and identify the ideal color scheme.

IKEA is not the only retailer taking the AR route to enhance customer experience. Wayfair, one of the world's largest furniture and home decorations retailers, introduced Decorify—an innovative technology leveraging generative AI. That solution empowers shoppers to envision their living spaces in distinct styles using shoppable, realistic images.

With Decorify, customers can upload a picture of their space and prompt the system to reimagine it in various styles like bohemian, mid-century modern, or industrial. The generative AI model then generates images showcasing the customer's room transformed to reflect the desired look and ambiance. Customers can explore different room designs and products within the application, making seamless purchases directly from the app. Additionally, users can select individual items in their rooms and have the AI model replace them with products from Wayfair's drop-down menu, further refining their vision.

If your products require a learning curve for new customers, an interactive user manual utilizing AR could be an excellent application. This innovative approach helps users grasp the ins and outs of the products by providing on-page contextual support. AR user manual apps often employ graphical arrows, animations, and text to indicate buttons in the real-life environment, making the learning process seamless and intuitive.

I love it when new technology bridges physical and virtual worlds and creates engaging digital experiences in retail stores. What Immertia.io is doing is not far from what we used to see in sci-fi movies just five years ago.

Its AR technology transforms product packaging into immersive, brand-driven experiences that consumers activate with smartphone apps.

Shoppers point their phones at a product, which becomes life in the app enhanced with video, images, or text information. The first-of-its-kind platform transforms any physical products into digital touchpoints, and it works seamlessly with existing products, which means brands can quickly turn their entire product range into a small army of virtual brand ambassadors telling brand stories and making new connections.

Source: Immertia

Augmented Reality in eCommerce opens new opportunities to engage customers and deliver captivating experiences.

Key Takeaways: AI-Assisted Shopping

Welcome to a new era when AI-assisted shopping will soon move from curiosity to functionality that modern shoppers expect. Technology is maturing, and Augmented Reality can help online Merchants close the gap with offline in-person experiences and provide a competitive edge.

I recommend eCommerce businesses develop a deep understanding of these technologies and not delay exploring how they can be deployed in their online stores to provide customers with interactive and immersive product experiences.

☐ Invest in Conversational Commerce capabilities by carefully selecting a solution that provides a genuinely interactive, Generative

47

AI-powered solution. Look for a solution that allows you to define brand voice and train it on your products and customer preferences.

☐ If you have already implemented chatbot support on the site, upgrade it to one that uses AI-powered conversational commerce and can maintain a human-like conversation. Old, rule-based solutions frustrate customers and reflect poorly on your brand.

☐ As the "conversation-first" future arrives, the bot's effectiveness will define customer impression of your brand, how much contextual value it adds, and how fast it can deliver it. The bot's capacity to engage in human-like interactions could lead customers to associate its limitations with the competence of the merchant's staff. Don't let it happen!

☐ Innovate with user interface and how to integrate Conversation Commerce into customer journeys. Be helpful, not annoying, test, learn, and adjust.

☐ Augmented Reality (AR) offers significant advantages to businesses selling online. By integrating AR technology into their platforms, merchants can provide shoppers with immersive and interactive product experiences. That boosts customer engagement and helps reduce returns by letting customers visualize products in real-life settings before purchasing.

☐ A special note to B2B merchants - your products are complex, and a knowledgeable virtual assistant can greatly increase customer satisfaction and conversion. You have a unique opportunity to leapfrog the competition by simplifying user choices with AR and knowledgeable chatbots.

☐ Merchants in the Fashion industry should plan to add virtual fitting room capabilities. They significantly impact the customer experience, so their adoption across the industry will be swift. Don't fall behind.

Generative AI to Improve Customer Service

"AI is like electricity was 100 years ago. It's going to change every single industry."

Andrew Ng, Founder of Google Brain

This chapter will explore opportunities to use artificial intelligence to process customer orders and provide post-purchase support. Integrating AI technology in post-sale processes within the eCommerce industry opens up opportunities for merchants to optimize operations and deliver better user experiences.

AI Tools to Revolutionize Customer Service

Generative Artificial Intelligence is set to revolutionize the customer service and support landscape. Technology research firm Gartner predicts[19] a 20% to 30% reduction in traditional service agents by 2026 as businesses adopt AI solutions to streamline processes. This technology boosts employee productivity by reducing customer request handling times and enhances interaction quality through reusable knowledge creation.

Generative AI tools are used to create chatbots and virtual assistants to handle a broad spectrum of customer support tasks. These AI-powered virtual agents can understand and respond to customer questions in a human-like conversational manner, making it easier for shoppers to find the information and resolve issues quickly.

By automating routine customer service interactions, AI will help businesses minimize human intervention and response times and ultimately lower operational costs.

A chatbot powered by conversational AI can use contextual awareness and analyze incoming customer queries to understand sentiment and intent. That means clients are more likely to get their questions answered the first time they engage and receive customer support, even during weekends and holidays with AI-powered chatbots. While a human support team is away, a chatbot can answer simple questions or perform common tasks, route customers to suitable knowledge base materials, or allow them to leave messages for agents and schedule callbacks.

While these bots are not entirely self-sufficient yet, they can answer most of the daily questions, allowing live support agents to focus on more complex issues.

Intercom[20] is one of the providers of customer service solutions that have developed a ChatGPT-powered bot. Its AI bot, called Fin, can understand complex queries, ask clarifying questions, and converse with customers in multiple languages. It also has built-in safeguards to ensure the bot answers questions based solely on support content, and Fin conversations are saved and can be monitored by the support team. Fin can triage complex problems and seamlessly pass them to the human support teams so customers get the best possible experience.

AI can adjust the response tone to suit each shopper, as some like an informal interaction, while others prefer more formality. In addition, AI can help agents by taking a short note written by a support agent and expanding it into a fully-fledged reply.

Order Management calls and chats are prime candidates for automation due to their repetitive nature and minimal requirement for complex critical thinking. To streamline these processes, businesses can leverage AI-powered virtual agents to handle routine order management tasks, relieving customer service representatives of these responsibilities.

Virtual agents based on natural language processing capabilities and integrated with Customer Relationship Management or Enterprise Resource Planning systems can efficiently capture order numbers and product names. By making API calls to internal systems, they can provide customers with accurate order status updates, deliver confirmation receipts, and perform various other tasks typically carried out by live agents.

By offloading routine order management calls and chats to virtual agents, businesses can enhance operational efficiency, reduce customer service response times, and improve overall customer satisfaction.

Virtual Assistants for Support Agents

AI systems will play a key role in enhancing the productivity of human customer service agents and improving support operations' efficiency.

When an agent takes on a case, it takes a lot of time and effort to understand the case's history, the status, and what has been accomplished by that point. Handovers slow agents down. AI can improve that process by creating a condensed summary of previous conversations and highlighting the remaining issues.

AI can benefit customer service agents by proactively suggesting the next actions to take. Through automated knowledge search, AI systems can provide agents with relevant information and recommendations, reducing average-handle-time and time-to-resolution and ultimately improving overall customer satisfaction.

Another area where AI can have a significant impact is automating ticket creation and routing. By utilizing AI, businesses can eliminate confusion and streamline the process of submitting support tickets. AI systems can automatically create support tickets when an issue remains unresolved or escalate an old ticket, ensuring customer concerns are addressed promptly. AI can intelligently direct these tickets to the appropriate person or department, preventing bottlenecks and ensuring efficient resolution.

These AI-driven technologies work in synergy to create a highly efficient support experience. By leveraging insights from past and ongoing conversations, AI systems continuously improve their suggestions for prompts and next-best actions, allowing businesses to gain critical customer insights and deliver personalized support.

Having a virtual assistant powered by AI is immensely valuable for support teams as it effectively handles a large volume of repetitive requests. That enables customer service reps to focus on more complex, high-value tasks requiring human expertise.

The virtual assistant is a force multiplier, boosting agent satisfaction, retention rates, and overall productivity. It empowers the team to handle a greater number of customer interactions in a shorter time.

To help eCommerce merchants utilize generative AI to compete on a level playing field, the customer support automation platform Kodif has built a low-code solution that empowers service teams. Kodif[21] offers two products using generative AI: AI Agent Assistant and Customer Facing Self-Service platform.

The solutions working together use conversational AI to answer service requests and queries for nontechnical customer experience teams. According to Kodif, it can address up to 80% of the most common requests. The assistant can also run analytics, providing insight into frequent problems and customer satisfaction scores.

Kodif offers specific use cases tailored to the needs of eCommerce merchants, such as refund, WISMO (Where is My Order), proactive outreach, subscription management, and risk and fraud prevention. These use cases address common challenges eCommerce merchants face and provide targeted solutions to improve support efficiency and customer experience.

While a common misconception of AI is that technology will take over a human's job, Kodif believes its tools contribute to better employee knowledge. The AI assistant trains agents to respond using the brand's voice in real-time. It's improving the agent's experience while simultaneously enhancing the customer experience as internal agents are now more educated and have better tools to respond to customers.

As an additional bonus, the onboarding time for new agents is also reduced. The chatbot can be integrated across various communication channels such as chat, SMS, and email, enabling it to interact with users on different platforms simultaneously.

Shopify has integrated AI across all parts of its system and found one more way to save merchants time setting up their stores. It always had a feature, "Suggested Instant Answers," that let merchants prepare automatic responses to commonly asked questions in the store's chat. That list is presented to the customer in the chat interface of the online store. The system shows the corresponding answer after a customer clicks on a question.

The enhanced "Suggested Instant Answers" feature uses Artificial Intelligence (AI) to generate suggestions for instant answers. AI is basing suggestions on the merchant's store policies and the store's conversation history. If there's insufficient information in store policies or conversation history, the suggested instant answers are based on common questions merchants receive—small but very useful optimization.

Multilingual AI Agents

Merchants can reach a broader audience and enter new markets by offering support in multiple languages. That fosters trust and loyalty among customers who feel valued and understood.

AI chatbots are multilingual and can help you provide support in your customers' preferred languages, leading to increased engagement and loyalty. By leveraging AI for multilingual customer support, brands can provide a high level of service without compromising quality or incurring additional costs. The human agents can focus on more complex tasks requiring expertise, while the chatbots handle routine inquiries in different languages.

Key Takeaways: Customer Service

Generative AI has tremendous potential to improve the efficiency and quality of customer service in eCommerce. From multilingual chatbots to virtual assistants to support agents, we already have existing technology that can make a great impact and should expect further improvements in the future. It is essential to understand that the goal of applying AI in customer support is not to replace support agents but to make them more efficient while improving customer service.

- ☐ Analyze where you have problems, long waiting lines, unclear responses, and focus on these areas.
- ☐ Set clear goals on what you want to improve and KPIs to use to measure the progress.
- ☐ Check what tools are used now and consult vendors on how they plan to enhance their capabilities with artificial intelligence.
- ☐ Understand the cost of implementation, including agents' training time
- ☐ Define types of support requests that are more prevalent and don't require critical thinking. Make them a priority for automation.
- ☐ Ensure the CS system is properly integrated with your CRM and ERP systems and can use APIs to retrieve required data like order details, customer information, and shipping status. That allows the Generative AI chatbot to use relevant information when communicating with customers.

Using AI to Gather and Process Customer Feedback

"Some people call this artificial intelligence, but the reality is this technology will enhance us. So instead of artificial intelligence, I think we'll augment our intelligence."

Ginni Rometty, CEO of IBM

Facilitating Customer Feedback

Customer reviews and comments hold valuable insights for retail and eCommerce owners. Statistics show that 93% of shoppers read online reviews before making a purchase, and an impressive 91% of individuals aged 18-34 trust online reviews as much as personal recommendations.

Yet, getting customers to write reviews can be a challenge. While they tend to find time for negative reviews, leaving positive ones feels like more effort to most people. AI tools can automatically generate review templates based on the purchased product and the customer's preferred tone and style to simplify the process. That streamlines the experience and encourages customers to provide feedback.

Or imagine if customers could simply dictate their reviews to their devices instead of typing them out. That would greatly simplify the review process, potentially encouraging customers to provide longer and more thoughtful comments. Voice assistants can play a role here as well. They can prompt customers to rate their shopping or support experience, allowing merchants to gather valuable information about perceptions of their service and areas for improvement. Voice review can then be used as audio or automatically converted using speech-to-text technology.

AI technology could also empower merchants to respond to customer reviews promptly with personalized messages. That saves sellers time and enhances customer trust by demonstrating responsiveness to their feedback.

What is important is that by using a powerful sentiment analysis engine, AI can accurately detect the sentiment expressed by customers and fully comprehend the content and intent of their reviews. Grasping customer sentiment holds immense significance for eCommerce enterprises aiming to continually enhance their products and services.

As part of Amazon's recent effort to incorporate artificial intelligence into more of its products and services, the eCommerce giant has launched an AI review summary aimed at streamlining the customer experience. Amazon's new tool uses generative AI to create review summaries, saving customers the time and effort to dig through swathes of user comments manually. The feature draws from the most frequently mentioned features and customer opinions and condenses its findings into a short paragraph on the product detail page. Shoppers who want more details can still go through relevant reviews manually.

By leveraging AI for gathering customer feedback, businesses can dissect customer reviews and social media comments, unveiling nuanced patterns and trends within sentiment. Such an approach empowers companies to preemptively tackle customer concerns, adopt well-informed choices, and refine communication strategies to align more effectively with customer anticipations.

Tackling Fake Reviews

In eCommerce, customer reviews play a vital role in establishing trust. Since users cannot physically see the products they intend to buy, they rely heavily on reviews and ratings from past buyers or users.

Sadly, knowing that not all reviews can be trusted is disheartening. Fakespot[22], an AI technology developer specializing in recognizing fake reviews, extensively analyzed reviews at active online stores on platforms like Shopify, Amazon, Walmart, BestBuy, eBay, and Sephora. According to their report, approximately 31% of online reviews are fraudulent.

Fortunately, self-learning artificial intelligence systems have made significant advancements in detecting fake reviews. These AI systems can analyze text patterns, writing styles, and formatting to quickly identify suspicious reviews. They can compare reviews in an instant and flag those that appear to be fake. That could be a game-changer for the eCommerce industry, enabling it to finally gain the upper hand in the ongoing battle against fake reviews.

Key Takeaways: Processing Customer Feedback

☐ Deploy AI tools to automate feedback processing and sentiment detection.

☐ Ensure quick response to reviews with automatically generated and personalized thank-you notes and feedback appreciation.

☐ Configure AI-powered systems to use sentiment analysis and flag reviews that require personal responses and create them efficiently using generative AI capabilities.

☐ If fake reviews are prevalent in your industry, invest in detection tools to flag them for human reviews and eliminate them when confirmed.

AI-based Fraud Detection and Prevention

And now, let's talk about a negative aspect of the eCommerce journey - online fraud. Online payment fraud is continuously on the rise. A study from Juniper Research predicts [23]that cumulative merchant losses from online payment fraud will exceed $343 billion globally by 2027.

Traditional fraud detection methods, often based on human-created rules determining what would trigger a transaction decline, are giving way to more efficient, AI-based fraud detection approaches. Rule-based fraud detection relies on policies that must prospectively predict impermissible customer behavior. That is cumbersome, inflexible, and frequently inaccurate.

Fraud detection AI, on the other hand, is most often based on unsupervised learning models, wherein large data pools from multiple merchants and payment providers and millions of transactions are analyzed by an algorithm. The algorithm isn't taught what to look for ahead of time; instead, the system finds insights based on behavioral patterns in the data. AI adds flexibility to fraud prevention and can spot anomalies and suspicious behavior without using pre-established rules. It can also provide decisions instantly.

In this way, third-party fraud detection technologies also enable more merchants to compete with massive marketplaces like Amazon and Alibaba. Fraud detection systems aggregate data from thousands of merchants and millions of transactions, putting everyone on even footing with giant marketplaces, both in terms of fraud detection and seamlessness of checkout experience.

As new behavior patterns emerge, AI-based fraud detection systems can adapt and make increasingly nuanced decisions. For example, in the early days of the pandemic lockdown, people who had never purchased home improvement items or tools suddenly made high-dollar purchases in those categories. eCommerce merchants had to adjust manual rues to avoid falsely declining purchases like these that would have appeared fraudulent before the pandemic. Fortunately, AI can quickly adapt to market conditions like these.

Expedited shipping is another excellent example. This shipping method tends to be a red flag in fraud detection since it minimizes the time a merchant has to cancel an order. However, expedited shipping became much more common during the pandemic, and the practice has become increasingly safe over time.

Suspicious payment activity can be especially hard to detect if it is perpetrated by historically legitimate customers. "Friendly fraud" is a typical example, and merchants are increasingly relying on AI to tackle situations where a customer disputes a payment with their credit card company to avoid paying for something they've already purchased from a physical goods retailer.

In these instances, the customer will claim an item wasn't received by filing a chargeback with their bank or credit card company. Some fraudsters even engage in large-scale chargebacks and sell items on the black market. That costs retailers millions of dollars each year, and if it occurred in a physical store, it would be classified as shoplifting.

There is also a rapidly growing trend in the form of policy abuse, which occurs when regular, paying customers break a retailer's terms and conditions to save or make money. There are multiple types of policy abuse. One of the most common is connected to refunds and returns. For example, a customer may contact a retailer to falsely report a missing item, triggering a refund or duplicate to be sent. Similarly, a customer might post a return to the retailer using an empty box (while keeping the original product) or send back used or worn items commonly referred to as 'wardrobing'.

Policy abuse is not the same as traditional fraud. Still, it has similar consequences for the retailer regarding its potential for financial loss — a fact that can sometimes go unnoticed by the retailers involved. In these situations, AI can spot sophisticated trends and patterns in the purchasing process to allow retailers to take action.

Fighting Sophisticated Chargeback Fraud

Chargeback dispute services use AI to gather data such as IP addresses, device fingerprinting, and behavioral analytics, then cross-reference this across past orders in the merchant networks. If the customer claims an order was fraudulent and not placed by them, the system can verify that it was placed using the same IP address and device where the shopper has placed orders in the past. That helps merchants prioritize disputes and tackle policy abuse from the greatest offenders. These services also automate the dispute process for merchants, making it scalable and more efficient.

As fraud tactics become more sophisticated, so too are fraud detection methods, which will soon go beyond purchasing patterns to analyze biometric aspects of eCommerce, such as "voiceprint" or the angle at which a mobile phone is held. These advancements will become increasingly necessary to protect customer accounts from fraud.

Consider this: a customer may exhibit abnormal ordering activity within a specific timeframe, provide false address information, or omit critical details necessary for successful delivery. These nuances are virtually impossible for humans to identify and evaluate in real-time.

AI models, on the other hand, possess the remarkable ability to swiftly develop complex rules that mitigate the potentially catastrophic consequences of fraudulent transactions. By leveraging AI, companies can shield themselves against attempted fraud, minimizing revenue losses and bolstering credit acceptance rates.

AI-powered engines can scrutinize multiple ID and credit card parameters to combat counterfeit or stolen information. This technology goes a step further by thwarting promo codes and loyalty program abuse. By detecting users with multiple accounts or those employing proxy servers for illicit purposes, AI ensures fair play and safeguards the integrity of online business.

For example, online fraud prevention services like Nethone[24] offer an AI-powered fraud detection solution and pre-trained machine learning models that can be customized using merchant data. The fraud prevention solution uses device fingerprinting, in-depth user profiling, and behavioral biometrics, all powered by machine learning.

Merchants must deploy AI solutions to stay ahead of fraudsters and protect their eCommerce enterprises.

Key takeaways: Online Fraud Prevention

In the dynamic world of eCommerce, fraud has emerged as a significant concern, with, according to Statista, a staggering $20 billion lost globally to digital fraud in 2021 alone. It's crucial for eCommerce retailers to implement efficient strategies to safeguard their financial health. Thankfully, the solution lies in the realm of AI. Through cutting-edge machine learning, AI can analyze millions of online transactions worldwide, detecting irregular and suspicious behavior patterns.

☐ AI has significantly increased online fraud-fighting capabilities.

- ☐ If your business is affected significantly, verify with your payment providers what steps are currently in place to identify and eliminate fraudulent transactions and their plans to deploy machine learning to further enhance these capabilities.
- ☐ Invest in more robust third-party solutions that process information about customer behavior on the site to identify suspicious patterns.
- ☐ Criminals also adapt quickly to new technology and can invent new fraud methods using AI. Merchants need to monitor this space and stay alert.

PART II
BOOSTING BACKEND OPERATIONS WITH AI-DRIVEN OPTIMIZATION

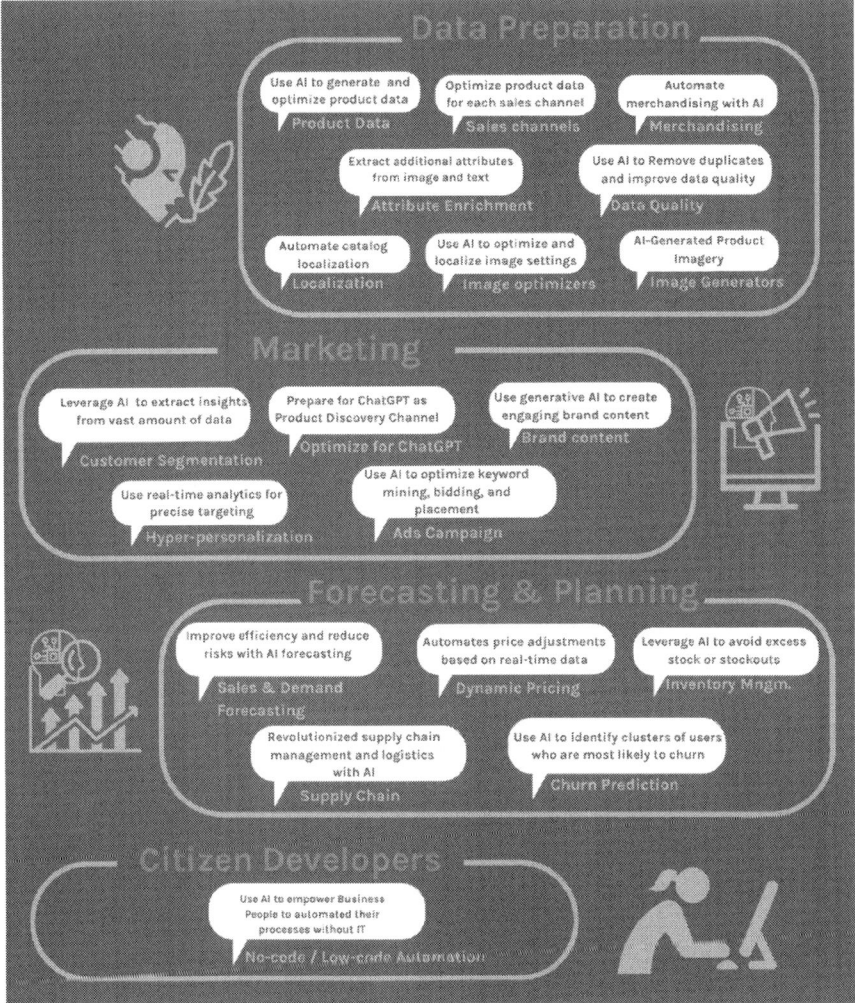

Data Preparation

- **Product Data** — Use AI to generate and optimize product data
- **Sales channels** — Optimize product data for each sales channel
- **Merchandising** — Automate merchandising with AI
- **Attribute Enrichment** — Extract additional attributes from image and text
- **Data Quality** — Use AI to Remove duplicates and improve data quality
- **Localization** — Automate catalog localization
- **Image optimizers** — Use AI to optimize and localize image settings
- **Image Generators** — AI-Generated Product Imagery

Marketing

- **Customer Segmentation** — Leverage AI to extract insights from vast amount of data
- **Optimize for ChatGPT** — Prepare for ChatGPT as Product Discovery Channel
- **Brand content** — Use generative AI to create engaging brand content
- **Hyper-personalization** — Use real-time analytics for precise targeting
- **Ads Campaign** — Use AI to optimize keyword mining, bidding, and placement

Forecasting & Planning

- **Sales & Demand Forecasting** — Improve efficiency and reduce risks with AI forecasting
- **Dynamic Pricing** — Automates price adjustments based on real-time data
- **Inventory Mngm.** — Leverage AI to avoid excess stock or stockouts
- **Supply Chain** — Revolutionized supply chain management and logistics with AI
- **Churn Prediction** — Use AI to identify clusters of users who are most likely to churn

Citizen Developers

- **No-code / Low-code Automation** — Use AI to empower Business People to automated their processes without IT

61

By applying AI-powered tools, businesses can automate manual and repetitive tasks to free employees to focus on more strategic activities and create a positive reinforcement cycle for the company and employees. AI-powered process optimization can reduce errors and increase accuracy, leading to cost savings and improved customer satisfaction.

We now have encouraging results from the first studies about the impact of generative AI systems like ChatGPT for actual business tasks. Three new studies tested very different types of users in different domains but arrived at the same conclusions. Productivity increased significantly, with the most significant gains recorded for the least skilled users. Some of the studies also found improvements in the quality of the work outcomes.

The studies were:

- Study 1[25]: Customer service agents resolving customer inquiries in an enterprise software company.
- Study 2[26]: Experienced business professionals (e.g., marketers, HR professionals) writing routine business documents (such as press releases) that take about half an hour to write
- Study 3[27]: Programmers coding a small software project that took about three hours to complete without AI assistance

In all three cases, users were measured while they completed the tasks: always for task time and sometimes for quality. About half the users performed the tasks the old-fashioned way, without AI assistance, whereas the other half had the help of an AI tool.

Users were much more efficient at performing their jobs with AI assistance than in the control group. Productivity was measured by how many tasks a user can perform within a given time — for example, a day or a week.

Here are the results[28]:

- *Study 1:* Support agents who used AI could handle 13.8% more customer inquiries per hour.
- *Study 2:* Business professionals who used AI could write 59% more business documents per hour.
- *Study 3:* Programmers who used AI could code 126% more projects per week.

These studies show us that even in the early days of AI technology, AI tools bring sustainable and measurable productivity enhancements. We should expect even better results when technology develops further and becomes more powerful.

But there is more. Improved internal operations will drive both top-line and bottom-line growth. AI will help your team create better product and marketing content and have more reliable information. That will increase conversion and lead to more sales and satisfied customers.

Optimizing Product Data Management

"We are now solving problems with machine learning and artificial intelligence that were in the realm of science fiction for the last several decades."

Jeff Bezos, the Founder of Amazon

We start by looking at AI's impact on the Backoffice operations of an eCommerce business and explore how AI can generate and enhance product data in an eCommerce catalog.

Catalog Product Data Explained

In eCommerce, online catalogs serve as the digital version of traditional store shelves. That makes a comprehensive, well-designed product catalog crucial for online businesses.

Let's look at what merchants must do to prepare product data to sell products online and how AI can make these processes more efficient.

Each product should be accompanied by a name, description, and one or even several images.

Each product category has specific attributes that describe them, such as color, size, style (for clothing), or memory and screen size (for computers).

Also, products have associated prices, tax codes, categories, and SEO data. If your business operates internationally, it becomes necessary to translate and localize this information.

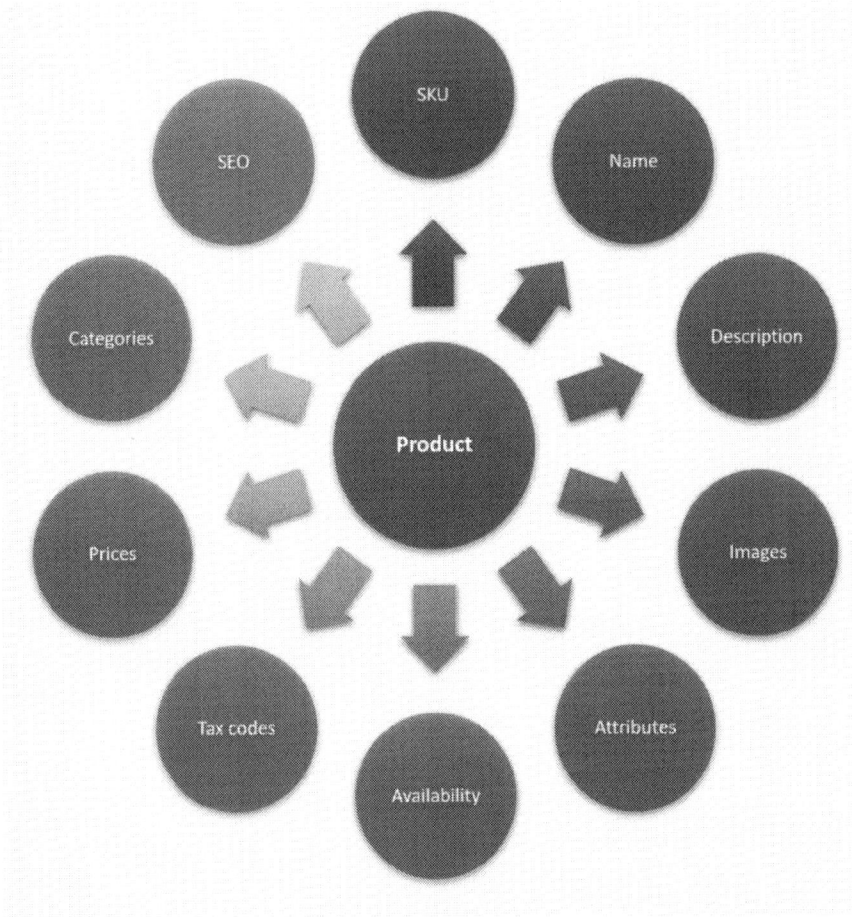

It is a lot of data to manage, especially for companies with extensive and often changing assortments.

Product Categories

To help customers easily find products, the Product Catalog should be well organized.

The Product Catalog taxonomy is the logical way of categorizing, grouping, and organizing the products. Proper naming and categorization and a well-defined set of searchable attributes minimize the time a customer will spend to find what they need. Well-done taxonomy improves customers' product discovery experience, which we will discuss in more detail in the Product Discovery Section of the book.

Merchants need to develop a deep understanding of their products and form a logical way to present them. For example, beds are made from Frames, Mattresses, and Headboards, which, in turn, can be categorized by their size and the materials they are made from. Multiple independent taxonomies can also be overlaid for different views on the same data. For example, a product could be found via genre or record label in a music catalog.

When the right product appears in a search, its purchase chance grows exponentially. Taxonomy organizes everything in the background to make that happen.

You might wonder why this can't be handled via the search bar. The answer is: If data is not well organized in the first place, the search doesn't work. It's the classic 'garbage in - garbage out' scenario.

A Forrester research[29] report found that poorly architected retailing sites sell 50% less than better-organized sites. Where searches failed, 47% of users gave up after just one search, and only 23% tried three or more times.

Conversion rates aside, taxonomy also has a significant impact on internal decision-making. Robust reporting and analytics are needed to know which products are selling well and which are not. As with any reporting system, good input is the key. Distinct categories and correct labeling make delivering accurate stats easier across an entire product catalog.

When it's clear what each product is called and where it sits, reports are more reliable, which leads to better decisions.

Many companies recognize the importance of a clean taxonomy and dedicate significant efforts to creating and maintaining it. And this work never ends. Taxonomies constantly change, especially in retail. Regular reviews and modifications of the existing structure should be a part of an ongoing effort. New ideas (like selfie sticks) will appear out of the blue and quickly become must-have terms. Adding product names, categories, and attributes never stops.

In large organizations, the taxonomy should be shared across business units. Customers don't have or want any visibility over the internal company structure. Merchants need to make sure everyone speaks with the same voice.

Managing a catalog is a lot of work, and we will explore below how AI can make this more efficient.

Product Variants

The same product is often available in various sizes, colors, materials, and price points. These purchasing options are product variants.

In the case of mobile phones, they will differ by color and storage size, so you are going to buy a blue iPhone with 128 GB of storage.

It is pretty common to have multidimensional variants. When modeling your digital products, the key consideration is deciding what to model as main Products and what to model as Product Variants.

Often, variants may have their own images, for example, to show a product in different colors.

Fortunately, AI has emerged as a solution to this problem, providing effective tools for managing and optimizing product data. Let's see how it can help increase merchants' productivity and quality of product information.

Using AI to Create and Enrich Product Catalog

There are multiple ways to integrate AI in creating and maintaining Product Catalog data. We explore here how Artificial Intelligence tools can help to write product descriptions, enrich product attributes, improve data quality, and localize the content.

Product Content Generation

Good and well-structured product data such as descriptions, attributes, and digital media have a compound effect on the revenue generated for eCommerce companies.

But even experienced copywriters can find crafting persuasive and SEO-friendly product descriptions challenging. The larger your inventory, the more time-consuming it becomes to write unique descriptions for each product.

But what if you could leverage the power of AI tools for this task? While human writers may still be needed for review and corrections, AI can swiftly generate engaging, distinctive, and optimized content based on your specifications.

Many AI tools now incorporate copywriting principles such as AIDA (Attention, Interest, Desire, Action) to emulate human writing styles. They can cleverly integrate keywords to ensure a natural flow of text. The easiest way to start is to use ChatGPT and copy and paste suggested descriptions into your eCommerce or PIM (Product Information Management) systems.

However, the market already offers a variety of AI product description generators that can produce plagiarism-free, unique, and SEO-optimized content for your catalog. You can choose from different templates, tones of voice, and languages to reach a broader audience. Bid farewell to writer's block once and for all while saving precious hours each day with the assistance of AI!

Let's look at some of the tools.

Product Description Generation with Jasper AI

Jasper AI[30] is an AI writing tool optimized for eCommerce that helps you easily create product content. A user provides simple inputs, and Jasper will generate original, high-quality content. Jasper can be used to develop various types of content, including blog posts, product descriptions, marketing copy, and more. Category managers can highlight product features and benefits using different tones of voice, keywords, and languages.

A user gives Jasper information about the product in the product description template. Jasper can generate several descriptions for one product simultaneously, and a user can choose how many variants she wants and then use the best from the list. Some descriptions can be short, others are more extensive, and users can control the length of product descriptions using Jasper's prompts. That is important if a merchant sells products on different channels, like marketplaces, which may have their requirements and limitations.

The tone of voice for generated content can be configured based on the targeted buyer's persona. It is an excellent option if the brand sells on multiple Digital Channels and has slightly different audiences in each channel. Changing the tone changes the produced output.

For best results, merchandisers should tell Jasper about the product's benefits to include them in the description. They can also ask Jasper to help generate a list of benefits based on a product's features and suggest several marketing angles to highlight them.

In the product description template, users should also indicate what SEO keywords to include in the content. And finally, you can save your product description templates as a recipe to reuse for similar products. Huge timesaving.

Shopify Magic - Generative AI for Product Content

Shopify Magic[31] is Shopify's catchall brand for generative AI. It includes a constantly expanding list of features that use AI to assist merchants in running their Shopify store. We will discuss different aspects of unique Shopify Magic functionality in the following chapters.

One of the standout features of Shopify Magic is its ability to generate content adapted to the needs of individual merchants. Shopify Magic can currently generate product descriptions in six languages, and you can expect that more languages will be added in the future.

As with Jasper, merchants can select a different writing tone for their content. If they are unsure which tone to use, Shopify advises experimenting with the tone settings to find a good fit for the brand's products and target customers.

The characteristics of the suggested content change to match the selected tone (Expert, Daring, Playful, Sophisticated, and so on). There is also a possibility to define and save a custom tone specific to the brand. The tone affects the output's vocabulary, sentence structure, and punctuation. It is recommended to maintain a consistent tone for product descriptions across the store. In addition to the Tone of Voice, merchants provide Shopify Magic with product features and keywords they want included in the description.

When users generate text for product descriptions, they can provide instructions directly to Shopify Magic to specify content length or format. For example, a user could add an instruction to write 40 words or less content, write the product description in another supported language, or replace some words with emojis.

Store owners communicate with Shopify Magic using simple text instructions like "Include emojis" or a more complex command, such as "Use regional sayings and slang from the American South". As Shopify Magic is built directly into Shopify Backend tools, no Copy / Paste is required. After users are happy with the results, they click the Keep button, and the product description is updated automatically.

We should expect more eCommerce vendors to follow Shopify's lead and integrate AI tools assisting with product data generation directly into their products.

For example, Amazon has debuted an AI tool for sellers that helps them generate copy for their product pages. Upon prompting sellers to enter keywords and a short description, it produces a range of content such as product titles, feature bullet points, and descriptions. Sellers can use the tool to create new listings or refine existing ones.

Product Attributes Enrichment

In addition to creating a category structure and text product description, merchants need to decide what attributes to use to describe different types of products and how they should be searchable and used as filters. Product attributes, such as color, material, size, brand, or weight, are displayed on the product detail page (PDP) and used in online store searches and filters. Merchants use product attributes to describe their products in a structured way, making it easier for customers to select what they want.

Incorrect attribute data can lead to poor search results and inaccurate product recommendations. That makes attribute enrichment critical for product teams looking to improve search and relevance.

To work with product attributes more efficiently, attributes should be grouped in the backend platform according to their character or specificity, for example:

- Physical attributes (e.g., size dimensions);
- Technical attributes (e.g., water absorption or density);
- Marketing attributes (e.g., SEO keywords);
- Logistics attributes (e.g., packaging type);
- And other.

For example, sneaker attributes are grouped into Composition & Care and Product Characteristics groups, while laptop attributes are grouped into Key Specifications, General, and Features groups.

Unfortunately, merchants do not always receive a complete set of product attributes from distributors or brands, and manually fixing incomplete product data is difficult. In addition to the process being manual and error-prone, it's challenging to decide which attributes buyers care about the most or where to focus the efforts. And small merchandising teams stretched to capacity feel these effects even more.

AI can help here with its ability to extract additional attribute information from visual and text materials using machine learning models for named entity recognition and image classification techniques.

Attribute Enrichment with Constructor

To solve the lack of attribute information, SaaS company Constructor [32]added AI-driven Attribute Enrichment to its product discovery tools suite. Its Attribute Enrichment engine automatically tags products with new relevant attributes and categories using deep learning and machine vision.

It offers diverse capabilities tailored to cater to various retail needs. Image recognition software can extract attributes from product images and add them to product data. For example, for a woman's summer dress already in the Dresses&Skirts category, Constructor can suggest adding it to the Spring Dresses category. It can also add additional attributes and attribute values. The color Rose can be added in addition to the Pink color, the Sleeve Type attribute can be populated with Short Sleeves value, while the Neck Type attribute will be set to V-neck.

Category
- Dresses & Skirts
- Mini Dresses
+Spring Dresses

Color
- Pink
+Rose

Brand
- AE

Graphic pattern
- Floral

Sleeve type
+ Short sleeves

Neck type
+ V-neck

Figure 1. Source - Constructor

Attribute Enrichment could combine raw product catalog data with buyers' behavioral clickstream data across touchpoints — correcting and auto-enriching product attributes to help buyers discover the items they'll find most attractive while improving personalization across their customer journey.

Consider a scenario where a shopper is on the hunt for a "Spanish red wine" on a grocery or beverage website. Attribute Enrichment comes into play by augmenting the existing product catalog data with valuable flavor profiles and regional information. This enrichment empowers the shopper to locate precisely what they desire effortlessly.

Attribute extraction could work as well for B2B products. Another example on the Constructor site shows a bolt getting a new value for the Head Type and even diameter determined by AI.

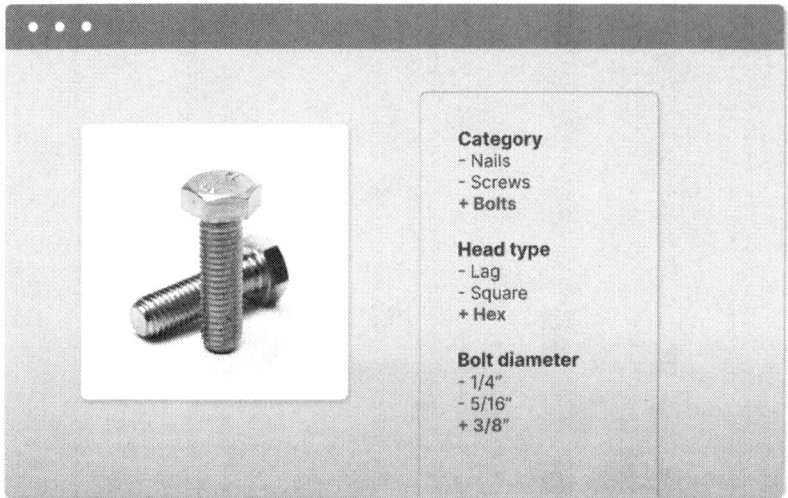

Figure 2. Source Constructor

Let's explore the concept of category enrichment through a construction supply website. Suppose there's an impact driver listed under the "tools" category. Attribute Enrichment's advanced algorithms analyze the product, along with its similarities to others, and automatically associate it with additional relevant categories like "power tools," "drills and drivers," and "cordless drills and drivers." This intelligent categorization simplifies the browsing process for potential buyers, ensuring they find the product seamlessly while searching, filtering, and browsing through the site.

Localizing and Optimizing Product Data for each Channel

To grow the business, merchants must offer their products in new geographical markets and channels.

But, before products can be offered in new countries, product content must be translated and adapted to a local audience. It is a complex, expensive, and time-consuming task if a merchant has an extensive catalog. In addition to translating products' titles and descriptions, merchants need to localize product attributes, change measurement units, and adjust SEO keywords.

And, to ensure that product content resonates with local consumers, merchants need to go beyond literal translation and adjust it to that market's cultural nuances and preferences.

Cost and efforts associated with manual localization efforts precluded many businesses from expanding internationally.

AI is a great democratization force that levels the playing field by reducing costs and empowering smaller merchants to grow their businesses globally. Several automatic translation tools on the market understand eCommerce and can do catalog translation at a fraction of the cost.

Product content could also require adaptation when opening a new channel. Language and tone that work great on a consumer site may perform poorly when selling to B2B customers.

Channels like marketplaces may have specific requirements for word count in product descriptions and titles and limitations on what words or expressions are allowed.

Expanding to new markets and channels requires an efficient automated process for product content localization, and merchants should look for software systems that use artificial intelligence to achieve it.

While enhancing a brand's global reach, it is essential to strike the right balance between localization and preserving the brand's identity. ChatGPT customization options are steps in the right direction, allowing users to define tone, audience, and brand focus to make generated content consistent.

Improving Data Quality

Many companies with large catalogs struggle with incomplete, incorrect, or duplicated product information. AI-assisted human annotation helps remove product duplicates or identical product variants, fix inconsistencies on product detail pages, and correct embarrassing spelling errors.

With accurate and rich product data, eCommerce teams can improve discoverability, engagement, and conversion in online shops.

Crossing Mind[33] offers an example of using AI for data quality monitoring and improvement. It constantly monitors the Merchant's catalog, assessing product data quality based on Competence, Accuracy, and Consistency, and recommends areas for improvement. Cluttered, disorganized product data causes costly mistakes and headaches and undermines customer experience. The AI-driven data cleaning service removes irrelevant entries, reorganizes data correctly, and deduplicates when appropriate. That leads to an organized product catalog that's easy to use and navigate.

Another artificial intelligence platform for data collection, categorization, cleansing, and enrichment is Unifai[34], recently acquired by the PIM vendor Akeneo. It reports that its customers have a significant reduction in manual efforts and improved accuracy in onboarding suppliers' product information.

Saving Time on Product Merchandising

The term Merchandising, rooted in retail, refers to activities to promote sales by presenting and positioning products in the store, like setting up window and in-store displays, grouping related products, shelf signage, and in-store ads.

This process is just as crucial in eCommerce stores, where the organization of products in online pages significantly affects revenue, customer experience, and brand interaction. There are a number of techniques used in eCommerce merchandising.

To highlight some products, businesses use labels like Sales or New, Best Seller, or Best Value.

Another popular merchandising technique is bundling, creating a collection of products sold together. Offering several related products together with a potential discount increases the order value and generates additional revenue.

Today, merchandisers spend a significant amount of time on manual tasks. And though these tasks are critical to eCommerce operations, they take away valuable time that could be spent on more strategic initiatives.

All modern eCommerce implementations use search technology to display products. Search engines are used to render Category pages and show customer query results. We will discuss the search in more detail in the Product Discover chapter of the book.

Let's now discuss Searchandising, which also greatly benefits from AI optimization. As you probably guessed, the term Searchandising is a combination of the words search and merchandising. In eCommerce, it describes how to influence search results to promote products when users search for specific keywords or phrases.

Merchandisers can reserve slots on category pages for a specific purpose, such as promoting products from essential suppliers. Searchandising strategies need to find a balance between multiple corporate goals, which makes manual adjustments difficult. For example, when placing products, the travel aggregator Booking.com needs to balance satisfying customer needs, revenue generated for business partners, and its margin.

To promote products, merchandisers manipulate product positions on search results by boosting their search ranking. And it's not enough to provide users with relevant results; the goal is to provide them with relevant results that the business wants them to buy!

We will discuss the modern search approaches and how AI can bring them to the next level in the second part of the book.

Automating merchandising and searchandising with AI involves streamlining various tasks, such as assigning products to the correct category, establishing product associations for upsell and cross-sell, determining search rankings, and uncovering new product connections. By harnessing the power of AI, these processes can be efficiently executed, saving time and ensuring accurate results.

AI algorithms analyze product attributes, customer behavior, and historical data to make intelligent recommendations, optimize product placement, and enhance the overall shopping experience. With AI-driven automation, merchandisers can focus their efforts on strategic decision-making and maximizing business growth.

With a deep understanding of natural language, today's Large Language Models (LLMs) will dramatically improve customers' intent understanding in search. AI can take customers' conversational queries (no more stilted language needed) and return far more relevant results. Those results are further optimized by merchandisers, whose business knowledge can marry what's relevant to customers with what's impactful for business success.

In regaining valuable time, merchandisers have the room to focus on relentless optimization, which will create endless new potential for business growth.

AI makes merchandisers more productive by offering conversational-driven merchandising. Backend users can start the process with requests like "Show me all synonyms for coffee table" and automatically add them to the site search engine. Eventually, they will be able to request things like "Create a merchandising rule that boosts all on-sale products in the Living Room furniture category with inventory coverage greater than 50%. Remove the rule at the end of the month." AI merchandising tools can also suggest and automatically create theme-based landing pages with top-performing products and content.

Particularaudience[35] uses AI to offer automatic product bundling. It optimizes bundle composition to ensure no irrelevant items are recommended.

Another company that offers AI-powered merchandising and recommendation systems is Crossing Mind[36], which we mentioned already when discussing improving catalog data quality. It uses Generative AI for product catalog enrichment by extracting attributes and tagging products to enable intuitive discovery, establishing cross/up-sell relations, and bundling products.

AI and Digital Media

In traditional retail, customers can physically interact with items before making a purchase decision. However, in eCommerce, comprehensive product information and images are vital in helping customers make informed choices. Research[37] has shown that the number of product images directly correlates with higher conversion rates.

So far, we have discussed generating and enhancing text-based product information. Now let's explore how AI can create, manage, and enhance Digital Assets like images and videos.

Retailers and advertisers face limitations regarding the quantity and quality of product photography required to create a captivating shopping experience. The costs and logistics associated with organizing extensive photoshoots, managing large product catalogs, and catering to diverse audience preferences can be overwhelming.

That is where AI steps in. Artificial Intelligence has the remarkable ability to generate virtually any image imaginable, opening up a world of possibilities for marketers and brand managers. With AI-powered solutions, creating new product imagery for ad creatives, campaigns, and social media becomes more efficient and accessible.

By harnessing the potential of AI in automating product imagery, retailers and advertisers can overcome traditional limitations, save resources, and deliver engaging visuals that captivate their online audience.

While the breadth and versatility of AI can be overwhelming, we will focus on two fundamental types of AI solutions:

1. Text-to-Image Generators: These AI systems can generate images based on textual descriptions, allowing marketers to bring their product concepts to life without the need for extensive photography.
2. Image Optimizers: AI algorithms that enhance and optimize existing product images, ensuring they meet quality standards, improving visual appeal, and customizing visuals for different platforms.

Text to Image Generators

Text-to-image generators are undoubtedly one of the most spectacular AI tools available. As the name suggests, they allow us to create a synthesized image entirely from scratch, using only a keyboard.

With this tool, we provide the system with a prompt, an instruction detailed in natural language describing what we want to create. In just a few seconds, we are presented with several options to choose from or prompt to generate further versions.

From the eCommerce perspective, Text-to-Image generators are particularly useful for inspiration, generating content for blogs and social networks, and overall communication purposes.

Merchants can use tools like Midjourney[38] to describe their imaginable products and create impressive, innovative images.

Here is an example of Midjourney prompts used to generate footwear images: "Design a line of futuristic footwear inspired by the sculptural and innovative designs of Rei Kawakubo, incorporating advanced comfort and wearable tech features" or "Create a pair of shoes with flowers on top of it, rendered in Maya, ultrarealistic".

While Text-to-Image generators offer exciting possibilities, it's essential to consider the unique requirements of eCommerce photography, where authenticity and accuracy play vital roles.

It is vital that the images accurately represent the product, as this builds trust and authority with potential customers. Achieving this level of reliability through Artificial Intelligence alone can be challenging. If the generated images don't closely resemble actual products, it can hinder conversion rates since they lack the necessary authority. Even more concerning, the potential increase in customer complaints and returns due to users expecting an exact match to the product based on the image can be pretty alarming.

AI-based Image Optimizers

Now, let's explore the incredible capabilities of AI-based image optimizers and how they can significantly improve our existing images. AI-based image optimizers are the tools that truly simplify our lives when it comes to the transactional aspects of image enhancement.

You might be wondering, how exactly do they achieve this? Well, the possibilities are truly limitless. Thanks to advances in artificial intelligence, we can achieve remarkable results that were unimaginable just a year ago.

Image optimizers offer a range of functionalities, such as changing image backgrounds, removing unwanted elements, transforming vertical images into horizontal ones by adding content, and even "raising" the resolution of low-quality photos. They can even automatically adjust image settings without requiring prior photography knowledge.

This software category is ideal for elevating the quality of merchants' image galleries and obtaining product photos that truly sell.

One such tool is Ecomtent[39], a SaaS AI solution designed for working with product images. With Ecomtent, merchants can upload a photo and describe a wanted scenario. The AI technology generates captivating lifestyle product images based on this input or can place product images in a new environment. For example, a merchant can place an existing image into a beach-themed composition and enhance it to create visually appealing images optimized for eCommerce conversion.

Visual content is pivotal in creating a strong brand identity and attracting customers. Generative AI provides an efficient, cost-effective solution for generating high-quality product images that align with the brand's style and selling channel. To effectively leverage Generative AI, businesses should define their brand's style and mood, carefully select relevant prompts, and continuously test and iterate their product images based on valuable customer feedback.

With AI product image optimizers, entrepreneurs and online retailers can access high-quality, visually appealing images without requiring extensive photoshoots or expensive equipment. As AI technology advances, we can expect even more remarkable applications in the world of eCommerce, making it easier than ever for businesses to present their products most enticingly and compellingly possible.

The Generative Personalization chapter will discuss more exciting opportunities for creating truly personalized images.

Key Takeaways: Product Data Preparation

The quality of product data and images is absolutely essential to success in eCommerce. These components are the cornerstones of conversion and revenue generation.

Creating, curating, and managing product information requires substantial time and resources. eCommerce merchants are not strangers to the effort required to keep product catalogs impeccable and appealing to customers. That is where the exciting world of AI steps in, presenting a golden opportunity to transform and elevate merchants' backend operations.

AI isn't a futuristic concept anymore—it's a practical tool available to merchants of all sizes. It's not about replacing the merchandising team but amplifying its capabilities. Online merchants need to think of AI as their trusty sidekick. It is here to ease the load and enhance product data quality.

Imagine a scenario where your team's valuable time isn't spent tediously organizing product information but instead brainstorming innovative strategies to drive growth. AI's potential to streamline these processes is undeniable. It can take over the repetitive tasks, allowing the product management team to focus on what truly matters—crafting memorable customer experiences and devising strategies to boost the bottom line.

Now, I encourage you to dive headfirst into the world of AI tools. Don't worry; you don't need a tech wizard on your team to make this happen. As we saw in this chapter, an array of user-friendly AI solutions is available, tailored to suit specific merchants' needs. These tools are designed to make life easier and operations more efficient, and we should expect even more powerful tools to be available soon.

It's time to embark on an exploration of possibilities. Start by experimenting with different AI tools and find the best ways to integrate them into your existing processes. Remember, the goal isn't just to adopt AI; it's to adapt it to your operations in the most effective way possible.

Take the first step by embracing curiosity. Set aside time to learn about the AI tools that align with your business goals. Explore their features, understand their potential, and visualize how they could transform your product data and image management. And, most importantly, give yourself the freedom to experiment. Test these tools, understand their dynamics, and observe the positive impact they can have.

AI journey isn't a one-size-fits-all endeavor. It's a tailored process that involves trial, error, and adaptation. Be open to tweaking your approach, fine-tuning your processes, and embracing the transformative power of AI every step of the way.

The potential to amplify revenue and operational efficiency is within your grasp. It's time to bridge the gap between where you are and where you aspire to be. Embrace AI as a partner and co-pilot on your journey to achieving outstanding product data quality and attractive imagery.

As you navigate the realm of AI, remember: It's not just about enhancing your product catalog; it's about revolutionizing your operations. The future is exciting, and the tools you need are right at your fingertips. Let's embark on this journey and turn your vision of elevated product data and images into a reality that drives your success.

AI in Marketing

"AI will affect every product and every service that we have."
Tim Cook, the CEO of Apple

Marketing stands to gain a lot from Artificial Intelligence from its ability to analyze vast amounts of data to understand customer needs, match them to products, and persuade people to buy. AI can revolutionize marketing strategies and significantly improve the marketing team's productivity.

Prime use cases for AI in marketing are:

- Smartly dividing people into groups using data analysis.
- Making a connection with each group.
- Crafting a unique personalized message to each segment based on its characteristics.
- Marketing content generation.
- Using ChatGPT-like tools as a new product discovery and marketing channel.
- And Ad Campaign optimization.

By incorporating AI into marketing strategies, companies can provide much more agile responses and unlock new efficiency and innovation.

Customer Personas & Segmentation

AI enables intelligent segmentation through data analytics, allowing marketers to precisely identify customer segments and form the basis for effective campaigns. AI-generated insights let marketers create new connections with customers and deliver customized messaging that resonates with their preferences.

First, let's discuss Customer segmentation approaches commonly used in eCommerce and the differences between B2C and B2B.

In the B2C, customer segmentation is usually based on:

- Behavioral data. That involves analyzing how shoppers engage with the brand and products on the website, social media platforms, and other channels.
- Geographical data. Factors such as country, region, postal address, and IP address can be utilized for segmentation purposes.
- Psychographic data. That includes aspects like lifestyle, personality, social class, values, and more.
- Demographic data. Segmentation based on gender, age, religion, education, income, marital status, or occupation.
- Membership. Memberships in shopping clubs or loyalty programs like Amazon Prime.

In the B2B space, businesses employ different criteria for customer segmentation:

- Firmographics. That is the B2B equivalent of B2C demographic data, involving segmentation based on business size, company location, industry, and other relevant factors.
- Customer tiering. Segmentation is done based on the potential revenue expected from customers or the most effective sales and marketing strategies to reach them.
- Needs-based segmentation. Grouping customers according to their specific product requirements or needs.
- Customer sophistication. This segmentation approach focuses on a target customer's awareness of the problem the merchant's products solve. It considers whether they are experienced users or newcomers who require education about the offerings.

Leveraging AI in marketing is a fundamental aspect that can significantly enhance segmentation strategies.

AI technology used to achieve it is called Predictive Analytics. Machine learning algorithms analyze historical data to identify and predict future trends. Companies use predictive analytics to analyze customer behavior and buying patterns. The goal is to identify potential customers, anticipate their needs, and personalize marketing messages.

Data can be analyzed without any prior assumptions or biases, such as that young males should be the primary target for video games while women are more interested in fitness products. Thus, AI can give merchants a far more accurate picture of their audience.

Many of those tools can also create entirely new segments by highlighting parts of the audience that could be overlooked by a marketing team, even if they worked on the same data.

With AI-powered customer segmentation, marketers can optimize their efforts, tailor messaging to specific segments, and achieve higher conversion rates and customer engagement.

Another important aspect of marketing strategy is defining Customer Personas.

AI tools are capable of utilizing a wide range of data, including psychographic, demographic, behavioral information, and qualitative psychological factors, to generate highly accurate customer personas. The analysis should include publicly available data and merchants' internal data to generate personas tailored to the company's specific needs. Some tools to achieve this are already available.

Companies like Delve.ai[40] use many data points from external and internal sources to create competitors and customer personas. These personas serve as fictional representations that closely resemble actual customers.

By gaining valuable insights from vast amounts of data, marketers are empowered by AI algorithms to identify specific customer segments with greater precision. This intelligent segmentation forms the foundation for highly effective marketing campaigns.

Marketing Content Creation and Curation with AI

As we discussed in the Product Data section of the book, AI offers powerful tools to help create various types of content, and it can also be harnessed in multiple ways to generate marketing materials.

Using Natural Language Processing models, AI tools can generate blog articles, social media posts, product descriptions, and email newsletters. Marketers provide prompts or keywords to the AI system, which uses its language generation capabilities to produce content aligned with the brand's tone and style.

Another opportunity is to use AI for Content Curation. AI algorithms analyze extensive data, including articles, blog posts, and social media content, to curate relevant and engaging content for a brand. By understanding the target customer groups and their preferences, AI identifies trending topics, industry news, and user-generated content that can be shared with the brand's audience.

By analyzing visual content, communication context, channel, and desired messaging, AI would help generate compelling captions and context for social media posts. That saves time for marketers and ensures consistent and effective messaging across social media channels.

And marketers are not limited to text only. AI-powered tools can generate visuals like images and videos for marketing purposes. For example, AI systems can create personalized product images by overlaying customer names or generate short videos using brand-specific templates and styles. It empowers visual storytelling and provides engaging content for social media, websites, and advertisements.

In addition to these opportunities, AI opens up intriguing possibilities in content intelligence. Understanding emerging trends and content distribution is crucial for forecasting demand and customer behavior. Using machine learning, AI enables trend detection by processing and labeling text posts, images, and videos. That allows teams to uncover microtrends quickly.

For example, an online business in the fashion industry can use image recognition technology to identify new fashion trends on Instagram. Human-in-the-loop techniques are then utilized to quickly act on emerging trends, uncovering growth opportunities for the business.

Advances in Artificial Intelligence offer many opportunities to streamline and optimize marketing content creation processes, ensure relevance to the target audience, and track the success of marketing campaigns.

AI Writing Tools Designed for Marketers

Let's look at two online AI tools designed to help marketers create engaging marketing content and increase productivity.

Anyword

A key feature of Anyword [41] is its ability to define a unique brand voice and use it consistently across all content created for a website, email, or social media platforms.

Once linked to a website, email, or social media platform, it automatically analyzes all the content rolled out on that platform and creates new content based on the best-performing marketing materials, audience, and other relevant factors.

For marketers or businesses without a landing page, Anyword can create one that aptly represents the brand. It can also take charge of all the postings the brand needs to increase its social media following.

With Anyword, marketers can also create Custom Scoring AI models trained on the brand's content and performance data to improve performance across all channels.

Through Chrome extensions, Anyword integrates with popular content creation tools like Notion, Canva, and ChatGTP to help marketers provide consistent writing everywhere.

WriteSonic

WriteSonic [42] is another AI tool for creating content that performs well in search engines. Its AI Writer generates fact-checked and well-researched content. It also analyzes competitors' websites and lays the groundwork for search-engine-optimized content. Writesonic positions itself as an AI-powered one-stop shop for all content needs.

With an increasing pace of innovation, we should expect more AI tools designed for eCommerce marketing to be developed and released in the future.

ChatGPT as Product Discovery Channel

Over the past few months, Matt Bahr, founder and CEO of the New York City-based post-purchase survey company Fairing[43], has been closely observing an emerging trend[44] that has caught his attention. When asked about the initial source of their product or brand discovery, an increasing number of customers have mentioned a new and intriguing factor: ChatGPT.

Although the frequency of these responses may not be overwhelming, it has been significant enough to capture Bahr's curiosity. As an astute observer of market trends, he understands that early adopters often serve as trailblazers, paving the way for a much larger wave of change to follow.

Bahr's realization that customers attribute their product awareness to ChatGPT indicates a more significant shift in how people interact with AI-powered tools in eCommerce. It signals a growing recognition and acceptance of Artificial Intelligence's role in the customer buying journey.

The implications of this trend are far-reaching. It suggests that ChatGPT and other similar AI systems are becoming an integral part of the product discovery process for a significant number of consumers. This newfound reliance on AI-generated suggestions and recommendations has the potential to transform the landscape of eCommerce, offering customers a more personalized and tailored shopping experience.

Optimizing Content for ChatGPT

So far, customers find products through ChatGPT by searching relatively open-ended queries. One response to a post-purchase survey for a jewelry brand said that the shopper had prompted ChatGPT to recommend a gift for his wife.

There are also examples of brands encouraging customers to use natural language conversation to discover their products. For example, the grocery delivery app Instacart will soon launch a new feature enabling users to ask natural-language questions like "What's a healthy lunch for my kids?" or "What are some easy options for family dinner?"

That may unlock a slew of new opportunities for retail brands to capture new customers. But merchants have to commit to playing the long game here.

While ChatGPT is trained on data until September 2021, Large Language Models are expected to eventually crawl the internet in real-time. That means that acting sooner rather than later is wise.

Although ChatGPT hasn't fully emerged as the go-to product-discovery channel yet, it holds tremendous potential for the future. To ensure your website is not intentionally blocking ChatGPT, you can utilize ChatGPT Plus in browsing mode and search your business's website. If ChatGPT says it's not available while still in browsing mode, visit an IP lookup site to find the user agent of the ChatGPT browser. Then, inform your site hosting partner or IT personnel to ensure the user agent isn't blocked.

By embracing AI-driven chatbots and optimizing the website, you can position your brand for success as the role of ChatGPT and similar models evolve in the product discovery process.

Businesses should ask themselves, 'How do we become a good brand for humans to find?' because ChatGPT emulates human behavior. If ChatGPT sees a specific item recommended as a gift in several articles by reputable publications, then it's likely that ChatGPT will also recommend that product.

To optimize for ChatGPT, you can extend the strategies that in-house SEO specialists at large retail brands are already implementing. That includes targeting longer-tail, high-intent, research-oriented keywords. To determine the best keywords for your site listing, think about the reasons why a product might appeal to customers.

Another valuable approach is leveraging Google to understand shoppers' questions about the brand's products. This strategy ensures that ChatGPT can provide more favorable results for your brand. But the real opportunity lies beyond search engines, anticipating the information customers seek and proactively providing it.

To effectively compete with large enterprises, smaller businesses should focus on filling specific niches rather than aiming for broad promotions. Instead of marketing a bicycle as the "best mountain bike under $500," it would be more advantageous to emphasize a specific use case, such as a "mountain bike for riding the Appalachian Trail." That opens up new avenues for smaller businesses to cater to specific niches and highlight unique product-use cases.

By understanding how ChatGPT functions and strategically optimizing brand content, a merchant can position itself for success in the evolving landscape of AI-powered customer interactions. It needs to adapt its SEO strategies to align with the ChatGPT capabilities and unlock the full potential of this transformative technology for its business.

Ad Campaigns Optimization

Artificial Intelligence can help to optimize marketing ad campaigns for maximum impact and effectiveness.

Imagine the convenience of setting up automatic campaigns that unearth the best-matching keywords for promoted products and smartly shift keywords between campaigns. This constant refining is a task that, in the absence of AI, would require constant monitoring and manual actions. AI empowers marketers to breeze through this process effortlessly.

AI doesn't stop there—it lends its brilliance to optimizing bidding strategies for paid advertising. It's like having a super-smart assistant that sets up an optimum course of action by considering various factors: historical performance, competition, conversion rates, and budget. The algorithms work their magic by dynamically adjusting bids in real time. That ensures that a business gets the most bang for its buck, whether it aims to maximize conversions within a specific budget or amplify the return on ad spend.

Consider this scenario: AI delves deep into data on keyword performance and ad placements, interpreting which drives the most conversions and cost-effectiveness. Then, it expertly tweaks bid amounts accordingly, letting you bid smarter and achieve your campaign goals with finesse.

AI doesn't just optimize bids; it's a creative genius, too. Using the treasure trove of ad performance data, encompassing click-through rates, conversion rates, and engagement metrics, it can uncover patterns that pave the way for enhancing ad creative elements. It could suggest tweaks to headlines, images, calls-to-action, and more, elevating the campaign's effectiveness.

Marketing tools powered by Artificial Intelligence can guide eCommerce marketing teams toward the most relevant segments for their online campaign, functioning much like an experienced eCommerce strategist, ensuring the resource allocation is both prudent and strategic.

Hyper-personalized Ads

AI technology completely changes how brands interact with customers, enabling hyper-personalization and automation in seconds for higher returns.

Merchants can deliver targeted advertising and offers based on search, browse, add-to-cart actions, and purchase history. Such advertising tools can contextualize the experience and instantly create images and videos showing products in locations and situations relevant to potential customer requests.

With targeted ads produced by AI, it is getting easier to catch prospective customers in the consideration phase. Online buyers hone in on their searches, and an ad might pop up, giving them precisely what they need.

Software that combines real-time analytics, segmentation, and engagement functionality enables marketers to adapt to minute changes in customer preferences at any moment instead of after the fact.

We will learn more about AI-driven personalization in upcoming chapters of the book, where we discuss how artificial intelligence will enhance customer experience.

Creating Marketing Content with Shopify Magic

In previous chapters, we explored how Shopify Magic's Generative AI[45] capabilities revolutionize product content creation. However, this powerful technology goes beyond that and also offers merchants the tools to craft captivating marketing content such as landing pages, articles, and emails.

With Shopify Magic, personalization reaches new heights. Whether it's generating blog posts tailored to specific events or customizing the tone of voice for marketing emails, Shopify Magic empowers merchants to deliver content that connects with their customers on a deeper level. Additionally, the platform supports content translation into different languages, enabling businesses to extend their reach to a global market.

When crafting a blog post, leveraging Shopify Magic is straightforward. The tool can generate both the title and the content for the blog, saving valuable time and creative effort.

To optimize the generated suggestions, merchants can provide the AI with essential details such as the blog post's goals, the type of information they want to share, and specific keywords—a huge time-saving.

Likewise, Shopify Magic is an invaluable asset for Shopify Email campaigns, making generating compelling subject lines and email body text a breeze. To ensure the best results, merchants must communicate comprehensive information about the campaign's objectives, product details, and specific keywords to the AI tool. Aligning the tone of the generated content with the brand's unique identity is equally vital.

To further refine the text generation results, merchants can incorporate the following types of information into their email campaigns:

1. Campaign type: By providing campaign specifications, such as product restocks, spring sales, or birthday discounts, the AI can deliver more relevant and targeted content.
2. Product keywords: For specific product-focused emails, including the product name and type, helps the AI generate accurate and compelling descriptions. When the product name is ambiguous, adding descriptive keywords or categories aids in refining the content or using Emojis to add a touch of personality to the message.
3. Important brand keywords or terminology: Provide AI with distinct, descriptive words to retain unique brand names and descriptions. Including brand names in brand tagline prompts can result in their incorporation into the generated content.
4. Other email details: Including relevant details related to the generated content type can lead to more effective suggestions. For instance, specifying the sale amount and the types of products involved in a sale message helps Shopify Magic suggest appropriate keywords.

By leveraging the power of Shopify Magic and providing comprehensive details, merchants can unlock a wealth of possibilities for creating engaging, personalized, and impactful marketing content.

Merchants using different eCommerce platforms need to look for similar tools that can be integrated and encourage their vendors to add AI functionality to their products.

AI-Personalized Videos

Maverick[46] is a SaaS platform that uses AI-generated videos to help eCommerce businesses create personalized customer interactions across their journey. With its software, businesses can record a single video and automatically personalize it for each customer.

Here is how it works.

1. Merchant records the base video (for example, a thank you note, a video encouraging a customer to return to an abandoned cart, or another type of personalized video).
2. Record a quick 15-minute script to capture brand voice.
3. Integrate with a CRM to select a customer audience you want to target and use customer information for personalization.
4. Maverick generates the videos, creates branded landing pages to host them, and sets up email delivery from your domain.
5. Once the videos are processed, Maverick will send samples for review. Once you greenlight the videos, it turns on the campaign, and the videos will start going out!

Virtual Host for Life-streaming

China's massive live-streaming eCommerce sector is known for peddling everything from lipsticks, food, and drink to smartphones, cars, and even a rocket launch service. It can easily generate tens of billions of dollars in sales overnight during major retail events like Singles' Day. Life-streaming shopping is also gaining momentum in Western markets.

Chinese tech companies started to leverage generative Artificial Intelligence to develop virtual hosts capable of round-the-clock sessions, intensifying the competition in this industry.

Generative AI involves algorithms like ChatGPT, enabling the creation of various content types such as audio, code, images, text, simulations, and videos.

The development of virtual hosts utilizes both 2D and 3D simulation technologies. While 2D hosts are more cost-effective, 3D technology offers better flexibility.

Despite the potential of virtual hosts in China's live-streaming eCommerce market, this AI application is still in its early stages. The adoption of virtual hosts is currently under debate; however, young people are likely to be attracted to digital personalities and embrace new technologies.

Virtual Influencers

While virtual influencers, sometimes called digital or AI influencers, have been around for a while, recent advances in Artificial Intelligence and visions of a metaverse have fueled their adoption and popularity. As their human equivalents, virtual personalities have a social media presence and interact with their followers from a first-person perspective.

These new developments open an opportunity for eCommerce marketers to use them as a cost-effective promotional strategy. AI-generated influencers have many benefits compared to humans, as they don't age and can be programmed to speak any language.

Ensuring transparency is the key as some virtual influencers are already presented as human-like, and it is becoming more difficult to distinguish between digital and real persona.

Key Takeaways: AI in eCommerce Marketing

As we finish this chapter on the transformative synergy between AI and Marketing in eCommerce, we can see how the fusion of technology and creativity opens new horizons for innovation and enhanced productivity. From customer segmentation to content creation, AI has opened many exciting opportunities in eCommerce marketing.

I would recommend the following steps in adopting AI in your marketing processes.

- ☐ Encourage the marketing team to use ChatGPT-like tools to brainstorm topics of marketing materials and generate draft content. Everybody on the team should become a prompt guru.
- ☐ Whenever possible, adopt writing tools specially designed for eCommerce to assist marketers in their writing and have functionality to maintain consistent brand voice and messaging.
- ☐ Assign a team member to monitor new product announcements of technological advances in this fast-moving field. Make sure that promising technologies are evaluated and tested. You don't want to fall behind your competitors in applying new AI capabilities and efficiencies.
- ☐ Talk to your existing vendors of marketing tech. to understand their roadmap and how they plan to utilize Artificial Intelligence to deliver new powers to your marketing team.
- ☐ Define the KPI for productivity savings you want to achieve by applying new tools and processes.
- ☐ Utilize AI to optimize and dynamically adjust advertising campaign spending and efficiency.
- ☐ Develop a strategy to optimize your marketing content for ChatGPT to ensure your brand is well-positioned for product discovery using large language models.

AI tools have become widely accessible, allowing merchants of all sizes to participate in this revolutionary shift. You don't need technical expertise; new tools are thoughtfully designed with marketers' needs in mind, enabling experimentation and exploration without limitations. Start using them, encourage experimentation, discover the tools that align with your requirements, and remain watchful for further advancements in this rapidly evolving landscape.

AI Models for Forecasting & Planning

"If you torture the data long enough, it will confess."
Ronald Coase, Nobel Prize-winning economist

eCommerce companies regularly use forecasting to manage inventories, plan logistics, warehouse space, and determine pricing strategies. Yet accurately predicting demand in an omni-channel environment is only getting more challenging because historical sales data are no longer enough, even when combined with seasonal data. Forecasting today is based on old and inefficient methods, which often leads to errors and miscalculations in capacity planning and supply chain assumptions.

AI-powered tools can help businesses analyze customer behavior and demand data to increase predictability, reduce waste, and optimize inventory levels. Let's explore use cases where artificial intelligence will have the most significant impact.

Sales and Demand Forecasting

Demand and supply volatility is one of the biggest business challenges in commerce. Fluctuating consumer demands can lead to inventory issues, missed opportunities, and potential loss of revenue.

Several factors need to be taken into account. First, analyzing sales trends over previous years provides a foundation for understanding historical patterns and seasonal variations. Additionally, projected or anticipated changes in product demands, such as market trends or shifts in consumer preferences, should be carefully considered.

That includes data points such as demographics, weather conditions, the performance of similar items, and even insights from online reviews and social media.

Finally, businesses should remain vigilant about potential supply-related issues impacting inventory levels, such as supply chain disruptions or supplier availability changes.

A tremendous amount of data to analyze, some of it constantly changing, makes excellent use case to apply artificial intelligence learning and forecasting models.

Unlike traditional methods relying solely on historical data, AI can also leverage real-time information to predict sales and demand. With machine learning capabilities, these predictions improve over time as more data becomes available.

Using AI algorithms for demand forecasting, eCommerce businesses can gain a competitive edge by efficiently managing their inventory, reducing costs, and ensuring customer satisfaction through reliable product availability information.

Particular Audience[47] specializes in applying advanced artificial intelligence technologies to eCommerce. Among other tools, it developed demand forecasting and analytics SaaS applications to provide merchants with multiple models of merchandise analytics.

Choice Modelling looks at optimizing assortment by looking at the sale rate of items against one another when both items are considered in a customer journey. At the same time, Dependency Modelling identifies items on whose availability other items sales depend to reduce amplified impact from out-of-stock products, while the Geo-local model analyzes stock distribution. Demand Forecasting is assisted by the stock depth and size depth analysis, with competitor price scraping and item gap analysis helping merchants identify gaps in their offerings.

Particular Audience offers good examples of how AI can be used to optimize forecasting and support buying teams in making merchandise migration decisions to optimize buy-online-pick-up-in-store and store-based fulfilments.

Optimizing Inventory Management

Efficient inventory management is crucial for online merchants to meet market demand while avoiding excess stock or stockouts. AI significantly simplifies inventory management by optimizing forecasting and enhancing decision-making processes.

There are three key areas where AI can make a difference:

1. Planning inventory replenishment: AI-powered inventory management solutions analyze consumer behavior and fulfillment choices to improve inventory levels. The customer-behavior-centric model needs to consider not just where but also *how* and *when* people want to receive their products.

2. Predicting estimated time to arrival: Providing accurate information to customers about the estimated arrival time of their products is crucial for meeting and exceeding their expectations. AI algorithms consider various inputs to improve the accuracy of these predictions, such as available-to-promise inventory and its location. This capability is especially valuable in today's competitive landscape, where customers expect guaranteed delivery windows, as companies like Amazon offer.

3. Safety stock management: Traditionally, businesses set static inventory levels, reserving a minimum par for walk-in sales, which is not factored into eCommerce or other fulfillment channels. However, generalized information is no longer sufficient with evolving customer expectations and the rise of omnichannel engagements. AI-powered systems enable dynamic adjustments to stock levels based on incoming demand. This automated re-balancing prevents tarnished brand loyalty due to unfulfilled promises and avoids the pitfalls of overselling or over-purchasing inventory.

To achieve profitable omnichannel results, retailers need capabilities that intelligently balance fulfillment costs against service levels. That helps enhance return on investment, improve customer experience, and increase repeat purchase behavior. Advanced AI solutions provide access to in-store and warehouse data, allowing businesses to go beyond linear, rules-based sourcing and meet seasonal customer and margin requirements.

Supply Chain Management

AI-driven tools offer several notable benefits compared to traditional supply chain management solutions. They streamline manual processes, minimize errors arising from complex supply chain dynamics, and assist supply chain managers in ordering the correct quantity of products at the right time. Because AI algorithms are based on calculating probabilities, they excel in managing not-fully predictable processes.

Here are the three primary use cases where AI can transform supply chain management.

1. Workflow Automation and Data Consolidation. Supply chain managers in medium to large companies often grapple with

managing data from various sources using manual methods like spreadsheets. This process is time-consuming and prone to reliance on outdated information. AI solutions can integrate with multiple data sources and automatically update the enterprise resource planning (ERP) system. That ensures data accuracy by submitting daily suggested purchases, transfers, and manufacturing orders.

2. Automatic Ordering Plans. Supply chain managers are constantly faced with questions about future sales, inventory levels, ongoing deliveries, and replenishment plans. AI tools will provide instant answers by dynamically simulating the collision of company schedules. These solutions automatically update ordering plans while considering demand and supply constraints. As a result, replenishment plans become more realistic and always up to date.

3. Dealing with Supplier Unpredictability. Supplier lead times play a crucial role in inventory management. However, supply chain instability can cause unpredictable fluctuations in lead times, disrupting inventory planning. AI tools promptly adapt to new lead times and automatically update ordering plans. That would enable supply chain managers to have an optimal purchasing plan ready for execution at any given time.

However, it's important to note that AI solutions do not make decisions or purchases independently. The current state of AI technology does not allow for complete autonomy, and processes must be developed to reduce but not eliminate human interactions and enable a review of AI recommendations before putting them into action.

Churn Prediction

As every merchant knows, retaining existing customers is paramount in eCommerce and direct-to-consumer businesses as it is less expensive than acquiring a new one.

To reduce churn, merchants can use artificial intelligence to sift through large amounts of data and flag segments of users that are at risk of leaving. With this knowledge, they can prioritize targeting customers based on the likelihood of churning and take steps to reduce the churn.

eCommerce AI tools like Churnly 48and Obviously AI [49]provide valuable insights into customer interactions across multiple channels, including email campaigns and websites. These tools continuously monitor customer behavior, enabling merchants to effectively identify areas that require improvement and tailor their strategies to meet customers' needs.

By harnessing the power of AI in churn prediction, businesses can take proactive measures to enhance customer loyalty and minimize churn by delivering personalized experiences, targeted offers, and proactive customer support, ultimately fostering long-term relationships with valued customers.

Dynamic and Personalized Pricing

In eCommerce, pricing decisions are influenced by multiple factors, including competitor prices, manufacturing costs, and customer demand. Conducting extensive research on these factors is time-consuming when dealing with a large number of products and channels.

What is dynamic pricing?

Dynamic pricing is an automated process of adjusting the prices of products in real-time to maximize income and other economic performance indicators. A dynamic pricing strategy determines the optimal price based on the current market state, including the company's previous prices, changes in competitors' prices, consumer preferences, time ranges, and other external factors.

For instance, Amazon monitors and updates its product prices every 10 minutes using the latest available data. Uber also employs a flexible pricing strategy to increase prices during high demand due to such factors as bad weather or a specific event.

Dynamic pricing algorithms use Reinforcement Learning models to process large datasets. By analyzing historic sales and price data, market demand, external events, and competitor pricing, AI generates a pricing model for a business that quickly adapts to changing conditions.

By leveraging the correct set of up-to-date data, AI-powered systems can predict opportune moments to raise prices or launch sales. This predictive capability empowers merchants to make strategic pricing decisions that drive customer engagement and boost profitability. It also enables personalized pricing, allowing businesses to tailor prices and offers based on the behavior of individual users on the website.

It is possible to adjust prices automatically based on global supply and demand dynamics. For instance, if a competitor's stocks are running low, the merchant can increase prices and capitalize on the urgency of shoppers willing to pay a premium to secure the product quickly.

Dynamic pricing has numerous benefits, including enhanced market segmentation, cost reduction, and maximized return on investment.

In addition, AI can streamline the pricing process by automating price adjustments for hundreds or thousands of products in the store. That saves time and resources that would otherwise be spent manually managing prices.

Research capabilities of different pricing engines and accepted practices of your industry to understand how to apply dynamic pricing in your online business.

AI-Empowered Backend Assistants

Shopify is launching a virtual assistant called Sidekick[50], which Shopify CEO Lütke describes as someone deeply competent, ready to help, knowing all the tricks in the book, and fully committed to your success.

I believe this is the most encouraging and inspiring example of AI's potential impact on an online business's backend operations. It opens exciting opportunities, and I expect other eCommerce vendors to start investing in similar capabilities.

Shopify Sidekick is a conversational AI assistant trained to know and understand all of Shopify. Sidekick acts as a virtual assistant for merchants, answering questions and performing tasks related to their business. Whether it's setting up a holiday sale or segmenting customers for a targeted marketing campaign, Sidekick has the answers.

Shopify Sidekick can assist merchants with various tasks, including setting up promotions and sales, segmenting customers for targeted marketing, summarizing sales documents, performing product research, and even modifying the shop design. It is a versatile tool that streamlines the eCommerce experience.

The merchant uses a simple chat interface to talk to Sidekick in natural language as it would with a trusted assistant who understands its business. A chat column appears on the screen's right side, and the chatbot is ready to answer any questions about the merchant's business and quickly accomplish tasks that consume too much of business owners' time.

In a demo video, Sidekick is shown answering a series of questions from a snowsports supply merchant in the Shopify demo store. Asked why sales dipped from March to July, Sidekick responds that it was probably due to minimal snow, serving a chart showing sales volumes month-by-month. It can answer a question about best-selling products and automatically prepare a report to back it up.

When the Merchant asks to "put products on sale," Sidekick suggests a 10% automatic discount on all products in the merchant's store. And it goes beyond just recommending an action. The user can even ask SideKick to create a discount rule. Sidekick automatically creates discount coupons and inserts a link to the report directly into the chat interface that allows the merchant to review it.

With SideKick, Shopify shows a genuinely innovative approach to using AI to empower merchants with a versatile virtual assistant. I expect other vendors to follow suit.

Alibaba [51]is adding a range of tools to help both B2B Buyers and Sellers on its marketplace platform. Its Smart Assistant serves as an intelligent personal research associate. It goes beyond merely asking questions in the chat; it functions as a personal expert to uncover valuable insights, recommend suitable suppliers, and prepare quotations. The Smart Assistant selects relevant suppliers based on buyers' requests and dispatch requests to these suppliers simultaneously.

And, to address cross-cultural challenges and language barriers, Alibaba now introduces real-time translation in 17 languages during live video chats, enhancing mutual trust between buyers and sellers.

Key Takeaways: Forecasting & Planning

In eCommerce, precision in forecasting product sales and managing supplies is a significant challenge. However, the formidable capabilities of AI offer a solution. Through analyzing extensive data sets and evaluating various scenarios, AI emerges as a crucial tool to optimize inventory and supply chain planning, predict churn, and apply dynamic pricing.

I recommend the following actions to unlock AI benefits in planning business operations.

☐ To take full advantage of AI data crunching and analytical capabilities, invest in consolidating available data across multiple backend systems to make them available for cross-reference and processing. Use integration tools like <u>Zapier</u> or <u>Alloy</u> that have pre-built connectors to various systems used by eCommerce companies to rapidly collect all relevant inventory and sales information and create a foundation for reliable planning and forecasting.

☐ Managing the backend operations of an eCommerce business takes a lot of effort. It is time-consuming, especially for organizations that sell in multiple channels and have a large number of products and orders. Virtual assistants like Shopify Sidekick can make a huge difference. Merchants need to start integrating backend staff assistants as they become available. Developing clear guidelines on their usage and training your personnel is essential. These virtual assistants streamline operations by automating various tasks, affording store managers more time to cultivate customer relationships and concentrate on strategic innovation.

☐ Explore how different AI analytical models can help your business with inventory and supply chain management.

☐ If churn is a concern in your business, invest in specialized tools to identify early indications of customers planning to leave and take preventive actions.

☐ If dynamic pricing could be used in your industry, invest in tooling to achieve and maximize the revenue potential it offers.

☐ Monitor your eCommerce vendor announcements for new AI features and look for add-on solutions that can be added to your technology stack with minimum effort.

☐ Be creative and persistent in exploring different opportunities to optimize your business operations and forecasting capabilities with Artificial Intelligence.

AI-Empowered Citizen Developers

"The purpose of artificial intelligence is to augment human capabilities, not replace them."

Satya Nadella, CEO of Microsoft

For as long as there has been software development, attempts have been made to make programming less technical and easier and involve business people without specialized training in automation.

You have probably heard the terms "no-code" or "low-code" and "citizen developers". Let's clearly define them and discuss what opportunities they bring to eCommerce organizations. Then, we will explore how adding AI to the mix further empowers non-technical people to take the lead in automating and optimizing eCommerce processes.

No-code defines tools that enable people to build programs and apps without conventional programming. They provide visual interfaces and guide user actions in simple to use and learn ways. They also offer pre-built integrations with other tools to exchange data as needed. If you've ever built a WordPress website or launched a Shopify store, you've already dipped your toes into no-code.

Low-code development usually includes no-code capabilities but also has the option to extend the logic with some scripting. These tools offer drag-and-drop editors, code generation, assembling a new app from existing components, etc. A good example is AirTable[52], which provides a low-code platform for application development.

With AirTable, non-technical users can build workflows to automate their business processes and harness the capabilities of relational databases to store and process data. More technically savvy users can use it to build complex formulas and script-driven automation.

The last term for us to define is Citizen Developer.

A Citizen Developer is any non-developer (a regular business user) who can tap into no-code / low-code platforms to build software for a specific business problem. In short, Citizen Developers are problem solvers. Their objective is not to build the "best" app but to design functional solutions to existing problems in their organization.

They understand business processes, are creative, and are comfortable leveraging low-code and no-code solutions to solve problems. They are tech-savvy and have excellent problem-solving skills.

Citizen Developers in eCommerce

There are a lot of different areas where business users use no/low code tools to optimize existing processes, automate data processing, integrate separate marketing and eCommerce systems, and even build relatively complex applications to manage their business.

Most small merchants start without any backend system like ERP and can get by at the beginning with the help of Google Sheets and Docs. But as their business grows, complexity increases, and manually updating all these long tables becomes a daunting and time-consuming task.

At that point, merchants start adding some scripts to automate the most tedious operations and create workflows that take several actions when a significant event happens. For example, when a new order is received, an SMS notification is sent to the shop owner, an order forwarded to the warehouse system, and an email confirming the order is sent to the customer.

A bit more tech-savvy merchants can switch to a more powerful low-code platform such as AirTable and use it to build a Product Management app, Customer Relation Management (CRM) system, or Inventory and Order Management. In AirTable, they can connect all of these apps together and significantly reduce manual work while not paying for expensive IT resources.

Every eCommerce business creates and processes a lot of data, which comes from and is used by multiple applications and channels. Not surprisingly, processing data and keeping them in sync across multiple applications is the most common task requiring automation. In most cases, a change in one application has a cascading effect and requires more than one step in fulfilling business requirements. That explains the popularity of low-code integration platforms like Zapier [53] or Alloy[54].

Zapier is an online automation tool with prebuilt connections to several thousands of popular apps, such as Gmail, Slack, MailChimp, Shopify, and many others. For example, a merchant can integrate with its email service and configure automation to send an email anytime someone creates a new invoice in the accounting system or when a new customer makes a purchase in the store. As a part of the same script, it is possible to add the customer as a newsletter subscriber in MailChimp (an email marketing system) and create an entry in the custom CRM system implemented in AirTable.

Zapier also added integration to ChatGPT, meaning many use cases for using Generative AI for content generation that we discussed in previous chapters can be easily integrated with other applications in your tech stack and be a part of catalog management or marketing automation workflows.

Alloy is using a similar approach to automation, concentrating more on systems used by online merchants and offering many eCommerce-specific templates to speed up workflow development.

Here is how it works.

Automation platforms empower merchants to design workflows and connections using triggers and actions. Each application offers an array of triggers and actions tailored to the service type. For instance, eCommerce platforms provide triggers such as "Order has been placed" and "Payment has been captured," along with actions like "Approve order" and "Apply promotion." Conversely, a transactional email service might feature a singular "Send email" action. By linking the "Order has been placed" trigger with the "Send email" action, you can automatically send an order confirmation email for every placed order.

Most modern eCommerce platforms are built following Composable, API-first, headless architecture. That makes it possible to connect them to the low-code automation platforms discussed above.

If a platform has an API, it is possible to automate a wide range of use cases, such as importing SKUs, prices, and stock data from an ERP/OMS system or validating and approving orders as soon as they are placed, which helps expedite the process.

AI-Assisted Coding

Generative AI can further expand opportunities for Citizen Developers. Low-code platforms are reaching a tipping point as generative AI is supercharging their use among business users who are not expert programmers.

ChatGPT supports coding much like it supports writing. The LLMs can generate code snippets and validate code in response to user prompts and parameters. It can write, review, and improve code without requiring extensive coding knowledge from the user. That is excellent news for Citizen Developers!

When generative AI and tools like ChatGPT are integrated within low-code/no-code tools, Citizen Developers can use prompt questions to describe what they want to build and have a chatbot create a skeleton code based on their requirements. All of this can be done without the need for extensive programming knowledge. When a generated code produces an error, a user can go back to ChatGPT and ask for advice on how to fix it.

If you cannot understand a complex code, you can ask ChatGPT to simplify and explain it. If you enter a code snippet in ChatGPT and ask where it is wrong or why it is not working, it will tell you the exact reasons in less than a minute. So, a task that usually took days for traditional app developers would become much easier with such generative AI technologies.

AI-powered tools can be used by citizen developers who have great ideas or insights but have little or no technical training. They enable them to drive technological innovation within eCommerce businesses. ChatGPT and other developer co-pilot systems are crucial tools to facilitate citizen developers' work and help them achieve coding goals that were once beyond their reach.

ChatGPT can also help ease the pain of creating user documentation for code. After you paste all the information related to your system into ChatGPT, you can ask it to document common questions and use the output for program documentation.

Key Takeaways: Citizen Developers

I don't see this area of AI capabilities getting the attention it deserves. Its impact can be huge in eCommerce organizations that constantly lack IT resources and struggle to survive on outdated tools and manual processes. It should not be like that anymore!

- ☐ Encourage the most tech-savvy people in your organization to start learning and using low-code platforms and ChatGPT capabilities to guide them. Their efforts will save you time by automating the most tedious and time-consuming tasks while reducing your IT expenses.
- ☐ Combine low-code tools with ChatGPT assistance to accomplish more complex tasks.
- ☐ Research available low-code capabilities and APIs in software used in your organization.

Conclusion & Recommendations

"The future belongs to those who can harness the power of artificial intelligence."
Mark Cuban, an American businessman, and investor

Throughout this book, we have explored the vast array of remarkable and exciting opportunities AI offers to supercharge an eCommerce business. While some of these ideas are still developing, tools available now can already benefit an online business. We have explored multiple ways AI will improve the productivity of internal operations and revolutionize the customer experience.

A new era is here for eCommerce professionals and entrepreneurs, with Artificial intelligence bringing powerful capabilities to even the most nontechnical users. It will profoundly shape how businesses operate in the future.

To capitalize and not fall behind the competition, today's whirlwind of activity must evolve into an AI strategy driven by the C-suite.

The rapid pace of AI development demands that companies prepare their business to seize its advantages. The future of AI is not a distant concept; it is here and now. It is time for us to roll up our sleeves and embark on the journey of building an intelligent and resilient business environment that harnesses the power of AI, all while staying true to shared human values.

With virtually every industry looking to scale operations through AI, the impact on ecommerce will be staggering. I believe it is now more risky to be a laggard than an early adopter. As Marc Andreessen astutely stated, "It's time to build."

Like the first businesses that grasped the power of SEO, those who now understand and implement AI techniques will have a competitive edge.

You have taken the essential first step by completing this book and gaining insights into AI's potential in the eCommerce industry. Now that you are finishing the book, you could feel a bit overwhelmed by the range of possibilities opened by these new amazing technologies and probably ask yourself:

-   What should I do next?
-   How can Artificial Intelligence benefit my business?

- Should I wait until new tools mature and are commonly accepted, or should I start ASAP, as there is no moment to lose?

As with all complex, multifaceted questions, the answer depends on where your business is in its digital journey, its size, technology sophistication, challenges, and the most urgent problems you need to address. But here are some numbers to keep in mind: it took Netflix 41 months to reach one million users, Facebook took 10 months to reach 1 million users, Instagram took less than three months to reach 1 million users, and ChatGPT achieved the same milestone in 5 days!

According to PitchBook Data, Inc. report, Generative AI's impact on the e-commerce ecosystem will likely materialize ahead of its influence on other sectors such as financial services, healthcare, or supply chain. That will be driven by less regulatory oversight and eCommerce's razor-thin margins that encourage innovation and experimentation. eCommerce merchants also sit on troves of first-party data from a growing number of online transactions that will power AI models.

Let us discuss the next steps you can take to supercharge your eCommerce business with AI powers.

Developing AI Literacy

"Artificial intelligence, deep learning, machine learning—whatever you're doing if you don't understand it, learn it. Because otherwise, you're going to be a dinosaur within three years."
Mark Cuban, an American businessman, and investor

The significance of AI literacy cannot be overstated. As businesses will increasingly rely on AI to elevate their operations, it becomes crucial for employees to possess a foundational level of AI literacy. That entails comprehending how AI functions, recognizing its capabilities and limitations, and understanding how it can be used in eCommerce and profoundly benefit the organization.

Every business must develop a solid understanding of fundamental AI concepts and gain comprehensive knowledge of use cases to apply AI in eCommerce. Introduce training, embrace a hands-on experience with AI tools, and promote a culture of exploration and learning among your colleagues.

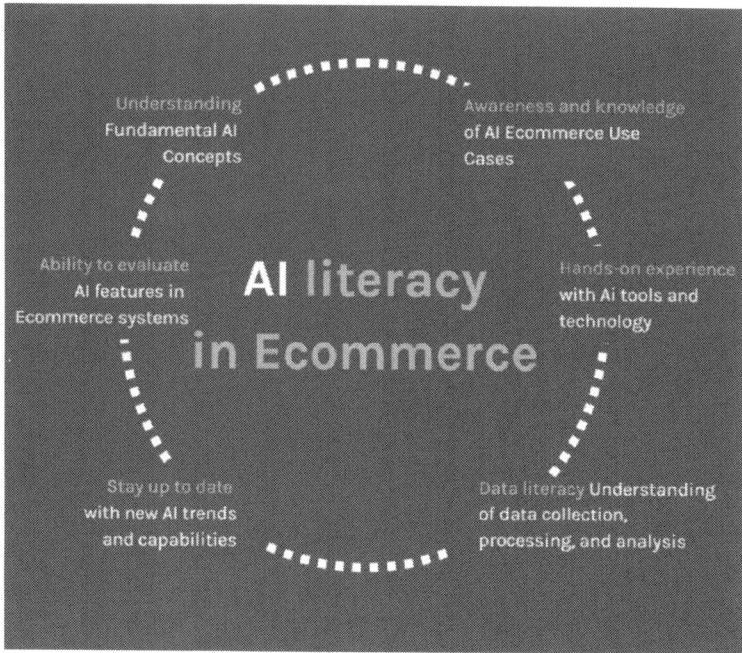

AI literacy in Ecommerce

- Understanding Fundamental AI Concepts
- Awareness and knowledge of AI Ecommerce Use Cases
- Ability to evaluate AI features in Ecommerce systems
- Hands-on experience with AI tools and technology
- Stay up to date with new AI trends and capabilities
- Data literacy Understanding of data collection, processing, and analysis

Source: CommerceIsDigital

Involve all the employees, from frontline salespeople to marketers, to merchandising team, up to the CEO, to go to these trainings, to get people to understand what data science is and what different algorithms exist for different tasks.

And then just let them play with it. Use classes for prompt writing. It's a new skill, very unlike typing a Google search. It's an entirely different way to think about how you interact with the machine.

By gaining AI knowledge, employees can identify potential applications of AI within their roles, collaborate effectively with data scientists and other AI experts, and make well-informed decisions regarding integrating Artificial Intelligence into their workflows. This knowledge and skillset will empower people to evaluate new features from eCommerce software vendors and discern which can benefit the business and when it is the best time to implement them.

eCommerce businesses must attract and cultivate employees who can determine when to use AI capabilities instead of human efforts, rapidly adjust to AI's integration into workflows, ask AI the right questions, and evaluate results delivered by Artificial Intelligence.

Continue to embrace a learning mindset as technology is constantly evolving. We are merely at the dawn of the AI journey, and by staying abreast of the latest advancements, you can remain at the forefront of this transformative field. Stay hungry for knowledge, embrace new developments, and adapt your strategies accordingly.

To stay on top of AI development in eCommerce, visit the CommerceIsDigital site to attend AI training and get ecommerce and AI technology updates.

Every Merchant Should Have AI Strategy and Roadmap

> *"Artificial intelligence is not the future, it's the present."*
> **Dave Waters**, Founder of AI Predict

Defining AI strategy and vision is paramount to your success. Now is the time to seize the opportunity and embark on your AI journey.

Given the multitude of areas where AI can revolutionize customer experience and enhance operational efficiency, it is crucial to formulate a well-thought-out plan of action. Begin by aligning your business goals with the AI roadmap. Identifying a specific business problem and linking goals to product performance metrics are vital steps in implementing AI for eCommerce effectively.

Narrow your focus on specific use cases that directly address your business problem and drive revenue generation or operational savings. By honing in on a well-defined use case, you can optimize the impact of AI in your organization. Do research and consider if technical solutions are available to achieve your goal.

Craft a comprehensive vision and strategy for leveraging AI to propel your business forward. This strategy should be anchored in the unique insights derived from your data, allowing you to differentiate your business from competitors. It is imperative to prioritize AI initiatives within your organization. Allocating ample resources and budget to AI ensures it receives the necessary focus and support to thrive.

Once your strategy, budget, and expertise are in place, it is time to take action and outline your projects. To expedite success, I recommend prioritizing relevant and narrow use cases that align closely with the insights derived from your data. Embrace pragmatism, prioritize effectively, and consider leveraging SaaS AI solutions for a swift path to deployment.

Having a capable team is essential for implementing a full-scale AI solution in eCommerce. Invest in AI literacy initiatives and seek advice from eCommerce experts to help you build an AI roadmap for your business.

Remember, AI is not a quick-fix solution; it is a powerful tool that must be wielded strategically to achieve desired outcomes. Keep this perspective at the forefront as you embark on your journey.

AI is fueled by data, much like how cars rely on gasoline. The most valuable data for AI often remains concealed within unstructured or flat files, with a staggering 80% of all data being unstructured and less than 1% currently being analyzed. To fully unlock the potential of AI, it is essential to take stock of the data available, involve data scientists, and devise a plan to unearth this hidden treasure.

Collect all data, even data that, at the current moment, you don't know how to use. Storage is cheap, and AI will most likely help you learn new insights from it in the future.

By defining AI strategy, assembling and training the right team, collecting data, and adopting a strategic mindset, you will be poised to harness the true potential of AI in transforming your eCommerce operations. Success lies in the technology and its alignment with business goals.

Artificial Intelligence opened boundless possibilities, and by taking action today, you can position your eCommerce business for unparalleled success in the future.

Additional Notes for Small Merchants

Small eCommerce enterprises are the brainchildren of exceptionally resourceful and courageous entrepreneurs who consistently cope with time and resource constraints while faced with numerous challenges from larger businesses.

Many people view artificial intelligence as primarily adopted by large enterprises with substantial resources. However, small merchants need to recognize that they have access to the same technologies and even greater motivation to make the most of these tools.

AI serves as a remarkable equalizer, evening out the playing field, and promises substantial rewards for those who embrace it early. That presents a unique opportunity for small merchants as AI can supercharge their efforts, enabling them to accomplish previously impossible tasks. The prime objective of using Artificial Intelligence is not to reduce staff or costs but to be more effective in marketing, eCommerce, and fulfillment efforts.

Small and medium-sized merchants need to realize that AI can be a catalyst for accelerating their growth, extending their niche, and innovating faster, enabling them to compete effectively against established e-commerce giants.

Choosing AI Technology

Selecting and adopting AI technology for an eCommerce business can be daunting, especially for organizations that lack the IT resources or expertise to develop AI solutions internally. However, making informed decisions is crucial when integrating new AI software into the existing technology stack.

Begin by exploring available tools that can be seamlessly incorporated into daily work without requiring extensive integration. For instance, leverage ChatGPT to improve product descriptions or marketing content or try other tools described in the book.

Evaluate the AI roadmaps of software vendors whose products you are using already. Assess how their AI functionality aligns with your needs. Consider becoming an early adopter by signing up for Beta programs, which can provide valuable insights and give you an edge in leveraging AI advancements. If your current vendor lacks AI capabilities in their product roadmap, it may be necessary to explore alternative solutions.

The AI boom has spurred the emergence of numerous startups focusing on various eCommerce use cases. If offered functionality aligns with your priorities, consider testing them and evaluating their technology for potential adoption. Ensure to assess integration options by inquiring about the availability of out-of-the-box integrations and APIs.

To get started, embrace experimentation. Do not limit yourself to solutions that provide only immediate return on investment. Sometimes, the most impactful experiments may yield exponential returns. Run multiple tests in parallel and carefully review the data to understand their impact on your business.

In addition to the above suggestions, here are a few more:

1. Seek recommendations and insights from industry experts or peers who have successfully implemented AI in their eCommerce businesses. Their experiences can provide valuable guidance and help you avoid common pitfalls.
2. Prioritize scalability and flexibility in your AI technology selection. Ensure that the chosen solution can accommodate your business's growth and easily integrate with future technologies.
3. At this early stage of AI development, avoid being locked in any solution, as new and promising tools can appear anytime.
4. Conduct thorough due diligence on AI vendors. Assess their track record, customer reviews, and case studies to gauge their reliability, expertise, and suitability for your specific requirements.
5. As most new AI systems don't work in isolation, evaluate how a new solution integrates into your existing technology stack. Check the availability of API and the technical expertise required to implement it.
6. Consider the implementation timeline and associated costs—factor in the upfront investment and long-term maintenance and support expenses when selecting an AI solution.
7. Require about customization options so you can adapt out-of-the-box products to your business requirements.
8. Establish success metrics and Key Performance Indicators (KPIs) before implementing AI technology to measure the effectiveness and impact of the adopted solution.
9. As businesses embrace AI, keeping ethical considerations at the forefront is critical. Make sure to evaluate the data privacy and security policies of a new vendor to ensure that the tool adheres to relevant data protection regulations, like GDPR, and doesn't expose your customers' data. Ensuring compliance with regulations in all business operations and being mindful of the human impact of AI in eCommerce are essential factors in building trust with customers, employees, and stakeholders. Select technology vendors that share these principles.

Final Thoughts

You've taken a significant step in understanding the transformative impact of Artificial Intelligence in digital commerce. As we conclude this exciting journey, I encourage you to keep your curiosity alive and stay vigilant in monitoring this rapidly evolving field.

AI's influence on eCommerce is just beginning; there's much more to explore. With advancements happening at lightning speed, it's essential to continue learning, sign up for training, and stay updated with the latest trends, technologies, and best practices. Embrace a growth mindset, and consider pursuing further educational resources, attending workshops, or engaging in industry conferences to deepen your knowledge.

The possibilities are limitless, and so are the rewards!

AI Terms and Definitions

1. Artificial Intelligence (AI): AI refers to computer programs capable of performing tasks that usually require human intelligence. It uses algorithms and data to simulate human-like thinking and decision-making processes.
2. Machine Learning: Machine learning is a subcategory of AI that trains computer systems to learn from data to improve their performance over time without human intervention. It enables computers to recognize patterns, make predictions, and act based on the learned information.
3. Deep Learning: Deep learning is a type of ML that uses neural networks. Its algorithms are designed to process vast amounts of data to discover complex patterns. Deep learning is used for such tasks as image and speech recognition.
4. Natural Language Processing (NLP): NLP allows computers to understand and interact with human language. It involves techniques that allow computers to process, analyze, and generate human language, making it possible for chatbots, voice assistants, and language translation systems to communicate with users.
5. Large Language Model: A large language model is an advanced AI system designed to understand and generate human language. It uses large amounts of data to learn grammar, context, and language patterns. Large language models, such as GPT-3, are trained on diverse text sources and can generate coherent and contextually relevant responses, making them valuable tools for tasks like text generation, translation, summarization, and even conversation.
6. Neural Networks: Neural networks are AI models inspired by the structure of the human brain. They are made of connected artificial neurons that can process and transmit information. Such networks can learn from data, identify patterns, and solve complex problems. They are commonly used in various AI applications, including speech recognition, computer vision, and NLP. Large language models, like GPT-3 & 4, leverage the power of neural networks to process and understand large amounts of text data to generate contextually relevant responses. Neural networks

provide the foundation for advanced AI systems by simulating the complex information-processing capabilities of the human brain.

7. Predictive Analytics: Predictive analytics involves using AI and statistical methods to analyze historical data and predict future outcomes. In eCommerce, they can forecast customer behavior, predict product demand, optimize pricing strategies, and recognize potential risks or opportunities.

8. Chatbots: Chatbots are AI-powered virtual assistants that can simulate human conversation. They are used to interact with customers, answer their questions, provide support, and assist with tasks such as product recommendations, order tracking, and troubleshooting.

9. Computer Vision: Computer vision is a discipline of AI that focuses on understanding and interpreting visual information from images or videos. It enables applications such as object recognition, facial recognition, and image-based search, which can be utilized in eCommerce for tasks like visual search and product categorization.

10. Sentiment Analysis: Sentiment analysis is the way of using AI to analyze text data and determine the sentiment or emotion expressed within it. It helps businesses understand customer opinions, feedback, and reviews, enabling them to gauge public perception and make data-driven decisions.

11. Personalization involves tailoring experiences, recommendations, and content to suit individual user preferences and needs. AI algorithms analyze user data, such as browsing history, purchase behavior, and demographic information, to deliver personalized product suggestions, offers, and targeted marketing messages.

12. Virtual Assistants: Virtual assistants, also known as voice assistants or smart speakers, are AI-powered devices that respond to voice commands and perform tasks. They can help with various eCommerce-related activities, such as searching for products, placing orders, checking order status, and providing customer support.

13. Data Analytics: Data analytics involves using AI algorithms to extract insights and meaningful information from large volumes of data. It helps businesses identify trends, patterns, and correlations in data, enabling them to make informed decisions, optimize operations, and improve customer experiences.

14. Data Mining: Data mining is the method of discovering patterns and relationships within large datasets. AI algorithms analyze data to uncover hidden insights and valuable information that can be used to drive business strategies, identify market trends, and optimize processes.

15. Visual Content Generation: Visual content generation refers to using AI algorithms to create or generate visual media, such as images, graphics, or videos. AI-powered tools can generate visually appealing content based on specific parameters or input, saving time and effort in content creation.

16. Visual Content Recognition: Visual content recognition involves using AI to analyze and interpret visual information, such as images or videos, and recognize specific objects, patterns, or features within them. This technology enables applications like object recognition, facial recognition, and image categorization.

17. Voice-to-text: Voice-to-text, also known as speech recognition, is the process of converting spoken words or audio input into written text. AI-powered voice-to-text systems analyze audio signals, identify spoken words, and transcribe them into textual form, making processing and analyzing spoken information easier.

18. Text to Voice: Text-to-voice, also known as text-to-speech (TTS), involves the conversion of written text into spoken words. AI algorithms analyze the text and generate synthesized speech that closely resembles natural human speech. Text-to-speech technology is used in applications such as voice assistants, audiobooks, and accessibility tools.

References

[1] CommerceIsDigital.com

[2] https://www.techradar.com/news/poor-quality-websites-are-costing-businesses-billions-in-lost-sales

[3] https://cloud.google.com/blog/topics/retail/search-abandonment-impacts-retail-sales-brand-loyalty

[4] https://www.forrester.com/report/MustHave-eCommerce-Features/RES89561

[5] https://www.klevu.com/

[6] https://www.sizolution.ai/

[7] https://www.visenze.com/

[8] https://www.outfindo.com/

[9] https://www.emailmonday.com/generative-personalisation-ai/

[10] https://www.letscooee.com/

[11] https://medium.com/chris-messina/conversational-commerce-92e0bccfc3ff

[12] https://corporate.walmart.com/newsroom/2022/12/14/text-to-shop-walmart-customers-can-now-shop-as-easily-as-texting

[13] http://getgrowai.com/

[14] https://www.freethink.com/robots-ai/virtual-try-on

[15] https://corporate.walmart.com/newsroom/2022/09/15/walmart-levels-up-virtual-try-on-for-apparel-with-be-your-own-model-experience

[16] https://geenee.ar/

[17] https://geenee.ar/ar_mirror/

[18] https://www.perfectcorp.com/business/showcase/watches

[19] https://www.gartner.com/en/newsroom/press-releases/2023-08-03-customer-service-and-support-leaders-should-assess-generative-ai-technology-options-to-enhance-their-organizations-function

[20] https://www.intercom.com/

[21] https://kodif.ai/

[22] https://www.fakespot.com/

[23] https://cts.businesswire.com/ct/CT?id=smartlink&url=https%3A%2F%2Fwww.juniperresearch.com%2Fhome%3Futm_campaign%3Dpr1_onlinepayment fraud_financial_fintech_jul22%26utm_source%3Dbusinesswire%26utm_mediu m%3Dpr&esheet=52775078&newsitemid=20220710005013&lan=en-US&anchor=Juniper+Research&index=1&md5=c4b0b0c46c87ed41e1f1803d86 88b0e2

[24] https://nethone.com/

[25] https://www.nngroup.com/articles/ai-productivity-customer-support/

[26] https://www.nngroup.com/articles/chatgpt-productivity/

[27] https://www.nngroup.com/articles/ai-programmers-productive/

[28] https://www.nngroup.com/articles/ai-tools-productivity-gains/

[29] https://www.bloomreach.com/en/blog/2019/08/product-taxonomy.html

[30] https://www.jasper.ai/tools/product-description-generator

[31] https://www.shopify.com/magic

[32] https://constructor.io/

[33] https://www.crossingminds.com/

[34] https://en.unifai.fr/

[35] https://particularaudience.com/merchandising/

[36] https://www.crossingminds.com/

[37] https://www.researchgate.net/publication/262236894_Is_a_picture_really_worth_a_thousand_words_-_On_the_role_of_images_in_e-commerce

[38] https://www.midjourney.com/

[39] https://www.ecomtent.ai/

[40] https://www.delve.ai/

[41] http://anyword.com/

[42] https://writesonic.com/

[43] https://fairing.co/

[44] https://fairing.co/blog/qotd-using-chatgpt-to-shop-for-ecommerce-products

[45] https://www.shopify.com/blog/shopify-magic-spotlight

[46] https://www.trymaverick.com/samples

[47] https://particularaudience.com/

[48] https://www.churnly.ai/

[49] https://www.obviously.ai/

[50] https://www.shopify.com/magic

[51] https://pandaily.com/alibaba-com-unveils-its-vision-co-creating-a-revolutionary-e-commerce-ecosystem-for-b2b-entrepreneurs/

[52] http://www.airtable.com/

[53] https://zapier.com/

[54] https://runalloy.com/ecommerce-automation/

Printed in Dunstable, United Kingdom